From Coolshade to Cowley Road

the story of
Mrs Icolyn Smith

ANDREW BAX

An environmentally friendly book printed and bound in England by
www.printondemand-worldwide.com

Mixed Sources
Product group from well-managed
forests, and other controlled sources
www.fsc.org Cert no. TT-COC-002641
© 1996 Forest Stewardship Council
FSC

PEFC Certified
This product is
from sustainably
managed forests
and controlled
sources
www.pefc.org
PEFC
PEFC/16-33-415

This book is made entirely of chain-of-custody materials

BOMBUS BOOKS

15 Henleys Lane, Drayton, OX14 4HU
www.bombusbooks.co.uk
www.fast-print.net/store.php

From Coolshade to Cowley Road
© Andrew Bax 2015

ISBN 978-178456-145-1

A catalogue record for this book is available from the British Library

First published 2015 by
BOMBUS BOOKS
An imprint of Fast-Print Publishing
Peterborough, England

Contents

Acknowledgements

I shall never forget the day when Icolyn first invited me into her home. I was a complete stranger about whom she knew nothing but, from the very first, she was open and frank in response to my intrusive curiosity. I was always welcomed with a cup of tea and we soon established a routine; it would begin with me reading back to her what I had drafted from our previous meeting so that she could point out where I had got it wrong, and we would then move on to the next aspect of her life, and more questions from me. We had many such sessions over the next two years and, now that the job is done, I shall greatly miss those afternoons in Kelburne Road.

I just hope the trust she put in me is justified by the publication of this little book. I realised from the very beginning that I had chanced upon a really exceptional person and the more I got to know her, the more my admiration grew. Putting together this account of her life from her childhood in rural Jamaica to her work among Oxford's homeless and needy has been a great privilege.

Not many people know her as Icolyn. To some, particularly her extended family, she is Miss Brown; others call her Mrs Smith or Sister; those who come to the Soup Kitchen address her as Ma. However, Icolyn is the name with which she was christened and is the one that has been consistent throughout her life. One of the earliest decisions we made when she and I began working together was that Icolyn would be the name we would use in this book. I have given fictional names to some of the other people it refers to in order to disguise their identity.

When I began to list those who had helped me fill in the gaps I realised that there were so many that I ran the risk of missing someone out. I have therefore taken the option of not mentioning any of their names, and I sincerely hope this expedient does not cause offense. However, those concerned know who they are; everyone has been generous with their time and patience, and tolerant of my endless questions. Their assistance has been invaluable and is greatly appreciated.

In 2013 the decision was taken to manage the Oxford Community Soup Kitchen through a charitable trust, The Icolyn Smith Foundation. There is therefore a structure in place just in case Icolyn, now in her 84th year, feels the need for a rest. All income from the sale of this book is being donated to the Foundation.

Andrew Bax
December 2014

1

A Stroll Down Cowley Road

OXFORD is known throughout the world as one of the oldest and most respected centres of academic learning. However there are many, lesser known sides to Oxford, including its diverse community of immigrants who have been drawn to live and work in the city. A stroll down Cowley Road takes you past shops and restaurants reflecting the cultures of ethnic groups from every continent; among its bustle you see complexions of every shade and hear people speaking in many languages as well as English. In Cowley Road there is one of Oxford's many mosques, attracting up to 2000 worshipers for Friday Prayers, and which was built entirely from public subscription. Among the organisations located here is Amnesty Welcome, a charity whose mission is clearly evident in its name and, in a business park at its eastern end, are the offices of another charity: Oxfam, committed to relieving the world's poor and destitute when struck by natural and man-made disasters. Outside the city there is an immigration detention centre whose role is often in the spotlight and sometimes controversial. So Oxford has many links with the outside world and the interaction between its very English origins and its new, multi-racial residents have enriched it and turned it into a cosmopolitan, modern city.

It was during such a stroll down Cowley Road that I realised how little I knew about the people around me and how different their lives must have been to my own. As a typical middle-class Brit I had not known real hardship and took for granted the usual comforts of the 21st century. What, I wondered, must life have been for the first generation of immigrants which, for whatever reason, had crossed

Shops in Cowley Road. Photograph: Kamyar Adl

continents and oceans to make their home in Oxford? I decided to call in at the Asian Cultural Centre to find out. There I hoped to meet one or two people from the Indian sub-continent and China who may be willing to tell me their life story as part of a book I was planning. Instead I met Icolyn Smith.

It was a Wednesday morning and the Centre was heaving. Not, I was surprised to note, with people of Asian origin, but mainly with Afro-Caribbeans, and the centre of activity was the kitchen. Huge pans were on the boil and near me a diminutive, elderly lady was stirring desiccated coconut into an aromatic stew. This was Icolyn Smith and for 22 years she had been running this weekly soup kitchen for Oxford's homeless who, ironically, were mainly white men. She was much too busy to talk to me but she invited me to contact her at her home. I learned that she had come from Jamaica in 1965 and that her great grandfather, who she remembered, was born in the aftermath of slavery. I realised immediately that I had found my story.

Jamaica! I had been there. Only on business, it is true, but I had extended my trip to visit a honey producer who kept his bees high up in the Blue Mountains. He also ran a construction company in Kingston's shantytown, which is where I agreed to meet him. The tensions which Icolyn experienced 30 years earlier were still apparent; my taxi driver refused to take me the last quarter mile because he feared his car would be stolen. So I walked, feeling pinkly conspicuous, between fragile shacks of corrugated iron and plastic, teeming with people in their many shades of brown and black. When I arrived I was greeted as if we had been old friends and immediately we clambered aboard an old Jeep.

Soon, outside Kingston, we turned onto a single track and into the foothills. It was hot and steamy and as the vegetation became

The Asian Cultural Centre in Manzil Way

thicker and more luxuriant, the signs of habitation became fewer; on we rattled and bumped. A couple of hours later, we stopped in a clearing, high up on a mountainside. Below us were rows of beehives, clearly very active, and beyond them the valley fell away steeply into misty depths. Further away tiers of mountain ridges rose above more mist-filled valleys, receding to the pale horizon in every shade of green, grey, blue and mauve. It was breath-takingly beautiful and I now realise that in getting there, we must have passed close to Coolshade, where Icolyn was born.

As I got to know her I realised that I had stumbled on someone who, through her remarkable dedication and energy, was providing a service of vital importance to people who were in the greatest need and, in doing so, she had saved many of them from destruction by drugs, alcohol or depression. Once I noticed a framed document and medal on the wall of her dining room. 'What's that?' I asked. 'My MBE'. Next to it was a photograph of Icolyn with Prince Charles. I still find it extraordinary that although I had lived in the area nearly all my life and knew Oxford pretty well, I had not heard of her before. She was clearly held in admiration and affection by many, including the hundreds – probably thousands – who, over the years, had been sustained and nourished in her Soup Kitchen. Some months after our interviews began I asked Icolyn if I could come along one Wednesday to help.

I arrived for kitchen duties at 10.30 in the morning; several other helpers were already there and I was surprised by the atmosphere of calm. Icolyn was standing at the gas range situated in the centre of the room, stirring something in a gigantic pan. Gloria, another Caribbean lady, was chopping vegetables and David, recently graduated from Ruskin College and a former beneficiary of the Soup Kitchen himself, joined me in doing not very much. Andy, a long-distance lorry-driver, strong, muscular and jovial, suffering in both knees and hips (he had an appointment at the Nuffield Orthopaedic Centre later that day) came down from the upstairs dining room where he had been setting the tables and chairs. Petronella and Leif, who is Danish, arrived and quietly went about doing what they knew had to be done; then Sylvia came, her contribution giving her new purpose after traumas earlier in her life. Gloria left and Diana came; in talking to her I leaned that she had migrated from the same parish in Jamaica as Icolyn but didn't know that before I told her. Then Marlon arrived, a tall, self-confident South African of Indian origin, who later confided to me that after a recent business failure it was Icolyn would dragged him out of depression. Somewhere in the middle of all this some crates of vegetables and other essentials were delivered by the food bank.

There seemed to be no planning and no rota; apart from Icolyn and a few semi-regulars, no-one knew who might turn up to help but, in the end, there seemed to be almost too many. Everything happened with unhurried efficiency and there was absolutely no doubt about who was in charge: the small figure by the cooking range, lifting the lids of various pots, giving their contents a stir and sometimes adding a bit of seasoning. Occasionally her quiet voice pointed out something that needed to be done, and it was done immediately. As twelve o'clock approached we gathered in a circle in a corner of the kitchen and held hands while Sylvia said grace. It was a simple, moving little moment.

Suddenly, for the first time since I arrived, there was co-ordinated action; everything had to be taken up to the dining-room. It was linked to the kitchen by a hand-operated lift which was only big enough to hold plates so the many pots and dishes had to be carried up the stairs. They were large, full and heavy, but small work for Andy. The soup today began as stock made from chicken bones that had been simmering all morning, into which Diana had mixed pureed vegetables; it was delicious. For main course there was a choice of lamb curry with rice or roast pork with all the trimmings. There were braised mushrooms and boiled cabbage and carrots but most popular of all were the roast potatoes – mountains of them, glowing golden and crisp on the outside – just as they should be. There were bread, butter and iced orange squash on the tables and, for afters, cake, tea and coffee. Although there was no way of telling how many people might arrive there was no shortage; indeed they were encouraged to come back for second helpings and to take some away for eating later; polystyrene boxes were provided for this purpose. As one craggy old regular told me later 'I've been coming for eight years and it's been a good meal every time – and that's the truth!'

The customers ('my people', Icolyn called them) formed a quiet, orderly queue; they knew the rules – they weren't even allowed in before twelve o'clock and waited patiently outside. At the head of the queue was a gaunt, unshaven character wearing a single ear-ring; he looked about 50 but Icolyn whispered to me that he was 35 and had been coming here since he was 17. Without her help, he had told her, he would have died long ago. Altogether there were about fifty men, of all ages, and four women, one of whom looked very poor and elderly, and had come all the way from Witney. Many sat silently alone, some in pairs and others in groups in which conversation became quite lively. Among them was an animated young man with wild, red hair; he had only just started coming; no-one knew why, or anything about him, but he told me he was Polish. I sat opposite

Everything has its place in the Soup Kitchen. Photograph: Harriet Browse

another person who had started coming only recently. It was difficult to tell his age, probably about 60; he was unshaven and shaking, and reluctant to speak. David told me that his world had collapsed after his wife's death; he wasn't looking after himself or paying his bills, and the bailiffs were coming in. It was clearly evident that everyone held Icolyn in great respect and affection; they called her 'Ma' and to some she really must have seemed like their mother.

I could only speculate what tragedies and destruction of self-confidence had brought these people here. The appearance of many betrayed their dependence on charity and the state for survival, and clearly most were unemployable. Some, however, were educated and articulate and one, who arrived late, carried a copy of the Times and was comparatively well-dressed. Had bankruptcy or divorce destroyed his life and self-respect? Then there was a big, hearty man dressed in a pristine white T-shirt. What was he doing here? Icolyn promised to tell me later. After they had eaten, some sorted through the donated clothes that are provided to those who need them, or took something extra from the food bank crates, or collected their polystyrene boxes for their next meal. Some dropped a few coins into a mug left for that purpose.

And then it was all over. They drifted away as quietly as they came; some stopped behind to help put away the tables and chairs; Marlon swept the floor and the rest of us carried everything down to the kitchen where washing-up was already well advanced. Everything was stored away in specially-locked cabinets, all the kitchen surfaces were cleaned and the floor swept. I looked at my watch; it was only two o'clock.

But the day's routine was not quite over. Just as we were packing up I heard voices in the passage outside. It was Christopher, talking to anyone who happened to be there. He had a cultured voice, charm and lively conversation and sounded much more sprightly than he looked; in fact he was a bent, frail old man. 'I come here for the company, not the food,' he kept saying, although he accepted a full polystyrene box. He was a man with a story, I am sure. We left him there, talking to Icolyn. It is how the Soup Kitchen ended every Wednesday.

2

Long Ago and Far Away

The indigenous population of Jamaica – and most of the Caribbean islands were Arawak Indians, whose numbers were decimated by European diseases when Spanish settlers arrived early in the sixteenth century. They brought in the first African slaves shortly afterwards but it was not until the British invaded the island and drove out the Spanish that the slave trade really began. Oliver Cromwell also used Jamaica as a penal colony, particularly for Irish 'rebels', including orphaned children, who were made to work the land. The main crop was sugar and, until the early part of the nineteenth century, Jamaica was the world's biggest producer. Decline followed the reluctance of estate-owners to invest in modern agricultural practices and new developments in sugar extraction; there was also competition from state-subsidised beet production in Europe. Gradually, the island's main crop became bananas. The economic collapse that followed the abolition of slavery in 1834 resulted in a shortage of labour, attracting emigrants from Ireland, Germany and France, as well as Britain. Indentured labour from India and China was also brought in, and Lebanese and Syrian traders followed. There is even a synagogue in Jamaica's capital, Kingston. All these races and cultures have blended into the unique Jamaican character, and very few people now have pure African ancestry.

Coolshade, in the parish of St Catherine is only about twenty miles from the bustle of Kingston but in the 1930s, when this story begins, it was a very rural, self-sufficient community of scattered, single-story timber houses with wattle walls and roofs made from thatch or corrugated iron. Icolyn Smith's family home was at the

Jamaica in relation to its other Caribbean neighbours

bottom of a ravine, approached by a track too steep for vehicles, and across a shallow stream which wound its way around the hillside. It was built on a slope so the front was on stilts, providing storage space underneath. Located in the foothills of the Blue Mountains, all the necessities of life were there: pure water spilled out from springs between the rocks, fruit and vegetables grew in abundance and chickens, goats, pigs and cattle thrived on the lush vegetation. It was a caring community; extended families not only looked after each other, but accepted equal responsibility for their neighbours: Coolshade did not know poverty or loneliness: hardship and good fortune were shared. Common values were shared too, including respect for each other and their Christian faith; on Sunday mornings the village was almost deserted because everyone was in church.

As Icolyn recalled her childhood and the care, happiness and plenty she enjoyed, it seemed a world away from the self-centred materialism that we consider normal in 21st century Britain.

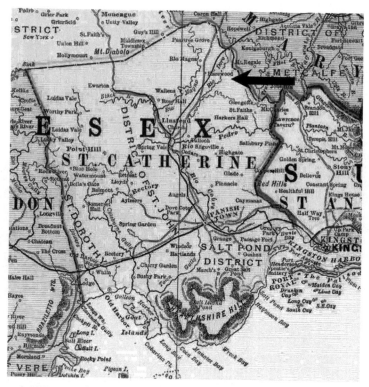

A 1927 map of St Catherine parish. The arrow shows the approximate position of Coolshade

One of her earliest memories is of her great grandfather on her mother's side, William Henry; he was born around 1860, within a generation of the abolition of slavery. He grew up during the period in which the sugar economy collapsed and, with it, the estates and fortunes of slave-owners. For much of the nineteenth century Coolshade had consisted of an estate of some 97 acres owned by a certain S. Stanbury but, as it fell apart, William Henry had acquired some of it and had became a 'cultivator', usually meaning the owner of a smallholding. By the time Icolyn was born he was living in a grand house, high on a hill with views down the valley below, surrounded by mahogany and cedar trees. Although it was a bungalow, the rooms were huge with a musty smell from bats that lived in the roof; Icolyn remembers other smells from the outhouse attached to the kitchen, where tobacco and cocoa beans were dried. William Henry's land may have been worthless once but he and his sons and grandsons cultivated it with care and expanded their property to five such smallholdings whose produce fed them all.

William's son Charles, born in 1888, married Maudryn Rigmayden in 1910, whose family was descended from maroons, groups of runaway slaves who established self-sufficient communities in Jamaica's mountainous interior and who had originally intermarried with the remains of the indigenous Amerindian natives. Maudryn was a dressmaker and one of her many children was Nelly, Icolyn's mother. Nelly's parents obviously had high hopes for her because she was sent to school in Spanish Town, an unusual privilege for a girl at that time. Their ambitions were dashed, however, when she became pregnant by George Brown, who was employed by Charles as a stockman, looking after his cattle and horses. One can only speculate on the domestic reaction to this event but Nelly and George eventually married although, by then, they had had seven children, including Icolyn.

Nelly was tall, like the rest of her family but George was small and feisty, like Icolyn herself. Although primarily a farmer, George also became a travelling barber, walking to nearby communities with his scissors, razors and brushes to earn some money, although most of life's essentials were acquired through barter. Sometimes he was away for weeks on end, following opportunities for work away from his neighbourhood, even travelling to other Caribbean islands if necessary. Icolyn believes her name originates from Cuba, not far away, and which he used to visit.

On some Fridays Nelly took the bus, or sometimes an open lorry, to Kingston with produce to sell in Coronation Market, returning the next day with family necessities including lengths of cloth for making clothes and the occasional luxury, particularly sweets for the

Icolyn's birth certificate, with her name spelled as Icolene

children. Despite the abundant sugarcane, sweets were highly prized and to make sure that everyone had their share, they would sometimes be divided by cutting into pieces.

Families worked their crops co-operatively, with barter as the usual means of exchange. Thus tomatoes might be swapped with sweet potatoes, eggs for cassava. Icolyn's uncle Alfred kept cows, so her family always had a bucket of fresh milk every day and, in exchange, he had whatever produce was available. And there always was a surplus: at the end of the day all the leftover fruit, eggs, meat and milk were fed to the pigs because there would be more tomorrow. That's why Jamaican pork is said to be so tasty and why Jamaicans themselves have such good teeth; they ate nothing but food that was absolutely fresh. Anything left over was bought for cash by travelling traders for sale in the markets of more urbanised communities. Labour was exchanged too: groups of young men might be cutting someone's sugar cane one day, someone else's bananas the next, and planting out young coffee bushes the day after. Successful agriculture depended on careful timing so that those crops needing plentiful rainfall, such as tomatoes and melons, would mature in March, May and October, the wettest months of the year; and crop rotation was practised to maintain the fertility of the soil. Jamaica's hot, steamy climate produced bountiful crops but, in the hurricane season they could be devastated by violent tropical storms. Icolyn remembers the horror of her father as he watched an entire hillside seem to split open and wash away his crops. But it didn't take long to have them replanted and growing again.

Life in Coolshade may seem simple and idyllic but, under the surface the strains which exist in every community were being felt by the adult population. Like most other countries in the world, Jamaica was affected by the economic depression affecting its main markets, Britain and the USA and, eventually, the chaos of catastrophic world war. Politically, movements for independence were also stirring, particularly in urban communities; traditional certainties were being challenged and the future looked less stable. It must have been a worrying time for people like George and Nelly with large families; although food was never a problem, they would have had a natural concern for their children's prospects. None of this would have been apparent to Icolyn as a child but she does remember it affecting her mother's brother, her Uncle Gilbert – a drinker, but a 'lovely man' when sober. He was violent to his wife but she was a big woman and 'knew how to look after herself'.

Whenever George was away from home it was his eldest son Ano who, in the Jamaican tradition and though not very old himself, took on the role of father-figure to his nine brothers and sisters. Within the family hierarchy, it became natural for him and his older siblings to be addressed as 'Brother Ano' or 'Sister Martha' as a mark of respect. Ano never left Coolshade; he worked on the farm with his father until his premature death at the age of 36, probably from cancer. He had five brothers: Eustace, who died while still a child, Colin, Mandley, Hedley and Seymour and four sisters as well as Icolyn: twins Martha and Mary, Viola and Enid. Boys remained subject to their father's discipline until they were 21; indeed fathers were often punished for their sons' misdemeanours; girls remained under their mother's control until they were about 20. Although Jamaican society is dominated by men, domestic affairs are very much the province of women; George used to refer to the house in which Icolyn, and all the family lived as 'your mother's home', an expression common in rural communities.

While boys were expected to help their father in the fields, their sisters would do the washing, cleaning and cooking in the home with their mother; meanwhile the younger children would do the

This house is very similar to the one in which Icolyn grew up – built on a slope and raised on stilts, with thatched roof and wattle walls. It is not known who this family is, but Icolyn recognises the style of home-made clothes, and lack of footwear

lighter work such as tending to the chickens and collecting their eggs, or gathering nutmegs which had fallen from the trees overnight. Chickens tended to lay their eggs under the protection of the fiercely-spined leaves of pineapples; indeed pineapples were used to define the boundary between fields and were as effective as any fence in stopping pigs from straying. The family rose with the sun and it was then, before the heat of the day, that many of the exchanges between farmers took place, with produce or cuttings of banana or coffee being delivered and received. So there was plenty of work for the children to do before they went to school.

Children's education began at home. By the time they were three years old they were expected to be able to recite the alphabet, count to ten and write their own name. Formal schooling took place between the ages of seven and fifteen. When the time came for Icolyn to attend Berry Hill School, over a mile away in Gubay, the usual procedure would be for her and the other pupils to walk there to arrive in time for a nine 'o clock start, back home for lunch and return for more lessons in the afternoon. However, on her first day the headmaster, a Mr Peart, invited her to stay at his house as a companion to his six-year old son. He was delighted by her lively personality and persuaded her parents to let her stay for two more weeks. Those two weeks were extended, and extended again Icolyn thinks, to over a year. It was an unusual arrangement and Icolyn very much wanted to be at home, but her parents acquiesced, probably because it enabled her to widen her experience. In any case, she still saw her sisters every day at school and home was not far away, so she was never cut off from her family. The Pearts were cultured, professional people and had a car with which they toured the island, so Icolyn saw much more of the country than most of her contemporaries. However, Mr Peart later took up a new teaching post in the parish of Manchester, some 50 miles away and although he and his wife wanted to take Icolyn with them, her parents decided that she should stay at home.

The school day began with all the pupils standing in line for an inspection to make sure they were clean and tidy, and to shake hands with the teachers. For their parents it was a matter of pride that their children's clothes should always be clean at school, and washing them every day was part of the routine. Teachers were treated with proper deference and when they entered the classroom all the pupils would stand in respectful silence. Although discipline was strict, the children behaved like children everywhere and exuberance and high spirits could sometimes lead to bullying, something which Icolyn experienced occasionally because she was so small, but she soon learned to fight back. She was a lively, mischievous girl, always playing tricks and, looking back on her school days, she believes they were among the happiest of her life.

There were just four teachers in the school and the main subjects were reading, arithmetic, Bible studies and Jamaican history. Unflinchingly, they learned about the slavery of earlier generations and how they had been exploited and ill-treated. On Thursdays boys were taught workshop skills and girls learned the domestic arts of home-making; on Sundays it was back again for compulsory Sunday school. Girls also had to learn about basic health care because the nearest dispensary was five miles away in Linstead and there were few hospitals outside Kingston. Women helped each other in childbirth and acquired the knowledge through practice.

There was no electricity in Coolshade but when the sun went down the houses were lit by oil lamps. Entertainment had to be home-made and there was always music and dancing. Icolyn's father played the mouth organ and the fife, which he made himself, and others would join in singing or making music on anything that came to hand. Icolyn has fond memories of dancing in the yard at night, with only the Moon for light. In her grandfather's home there was a full organ, powered by foot-operated pumps and she remembers with relish the powerful sound it made. If young people went out to a dance, a strict protocol had to be observed. Icolyn always had to be accompanied by an older brother and if she was late back, it was the brother who got into trouble. Although entertainment was largely home-made there was a rum bar in Gubay, serving beer, Jamaican wine and, of course, rum. But its patrons were mainly men; no self-respecting woman would be seen there.

Back home the main beverage was 'tea' made from the boiled liquor of crushed sugarcane, usually drunk from cups made from the hollowed-out and dried fruit of the calabash vine. Crushing sugarcane, boiling the liquor and straining it was one of the daily routines. While still hot the liquor was poured into a cup containing the leaf of an orange, lemon or some other fruit or herb, flavouring a drink that was very sweet but delicious. Coffee was made from hot cane liquor poured over roasted coffee beans and was sweet but also very strong. And any liquor left over was, of course, fed to the pigs.

The focus of the week's routine was the church, next door to the school in Gubay, and Sunday was the day for dressing up. All the women had beautiful, hand-made dresses and men wore their one, carefully-preserved suit. Although Church of England, the services were unlike the cheerless, dreary affairs of the mother country. In Jamaica, the church was a joyful place, and services were alive with clapping, singing, dancing and shouting. Sometimes they were taken by ministers sent out from England and, accustomed as they were to a more austere ritual, one wonders how they reacted to the unrestrained expression of faith in their new congregation. Every Sunday the church was full to overflowing, even more so during times of special celebration such as the Harvest Festival, when it was lavishly decorated with every kind of produce from that fertile region. On Mother's Day, all the young children were dressed in white and lined up in the church to present their mothers with a little basket made from cardboard and cotton wool containing two eggs and flowers. Eggs were also part of the Easter ceremony and it was children, again, who took them to the altar. No work was done on Sundays; after church it was a day of rest, for visiting friends and family and for socialising.

In 1944 one of Icolyn's elder twin sisters, Mary, who by then was living in Kingston, came home pregnant. George and Nelly were appalled, even more so after the birth and Mary returned to Kingston without Monica, her baby. To make matters worse, Nelly was also pregnant once more, and gave birth to Enid at the same time. Although the two babies grew up as sisters Icolyn, still a very young teenager herself, left school prematurely to look after Monica. It was a very distressing time, particularly because Monica's father wanted nothing to do with his child. Icolyn recalls everything becoming 'such a muddle'. Four years later, Icolyn herself left for Kingston, and Monica now lives in Brixton.

During those years of premature domesticity she went to work part-time for a neighbour where she perfected her skills in dress-making. Making clothes was a valuable skill and one which Icolyn put to good use later on. There was a constant need for new clothes and for repairing old ones; one set was used for wearing in the house and a different set for wearing outside or for work. Girls had few opportunities for further education or professional work so their prospects were mainly marriage, motherhood and home-making.

3

From Coolshade to Kingston

When Icolyn was eighteen years old she left Coolshade to join Mary in Kingston. Many in the family eventually moved to Kingston in the search for work and prospects, including her brothers Colin, Mandley and Hedley and her sister Enid.

Icolyn found work as a maid, or housekeeper, and her first job paid her two shillings a week – good money for someone so young, but she was strong and used to hard work so she did well. During the next few years she was employed by several families, mainly professional people; sometimes they had young children who needed looking after though often the children were older and, perhaps, at boarding school. Not for the first time, Icolyn's small stature was to her advantage; her employers were often beguiled by her exuberance and charm and treated her as if she was still a little girl. She took full advantage of her freedom and had 'a really good time', but her strict upbringing still had influence over her and, for example, she still felt unable to go dancing unaccompanied. However, life in Kingston was busy and exciting and, once away from the weekly routine in Coolshade, the church dropped out of her life, and she did not find it again until she was settled in Oxford.

Icolyn enjoyed an active social life and, after a while, she met Eric who lived in the same house as her sister Mary; unlike Icolyn, he was tall and quiet. It was not long before Icolyn found she was expecting a baby and her father, George, reacted with the same outrage as he had done with Mary. As far as he was concerned this was not the right sequence of events and there was an almighty rumpus – 'You would think I had committed murder!' Icolyn remembers with a laugh. Nelly was much more philosophical about it and, with help from her uncle Alfred, George was calmed down. It was not at all unusual for this to happen in Jamaica and, ironically, Icolyn herself – and all her older siblings – were born before their parents were married. Their baby was born on 28 March 1951 and christened Norman, and Nelly came to look after her daughter and grandson for two weeks after the birth. Icolyn and Eric were married on a weekday a couple of years later in a modest little ceremony in the local registry office; she was dressed demurely in white and Eric wore a black suit. They were attended by Icolyn's mother, her sisters, the children of course, and one or two of their female neighbours; in Jamaica, marriage is regarded as a domestic event in which men, apart from the groom, have little part to play.

The real celebration was held the following Saturday, in the yard outside their house. The day began early as female friends and neighbours brought food and helped with the cooking. A canopy was made from palm leaves as decoration and to offer some protection in case it rained. As guests began to arrive, dressed in their brightest and best, rum was served to the men and soft drinks to the women and children, and while the sun was still high in the sky the party was in full swing. Two of Icolyn's friends made speeches while their men looked on. Then some of the men took up their home-made guitars, fifes, tambourines and drums; there was a saxophone as well and maybe a trumpet. Soon the whole neighbourhood was alive with improvised blue beat and the exotic rhythms of the Caribbean. Music, dancing, singing and laughter went on late into the night and into the next morning, and as the last stragglers left for home, the sun was rising again.

Eric made a living by collecting, or buying used glass bottles, and recycling them; in the mango season he sold the fleshy fruit from a cart and, in between times, he did odd jobs as a carpenter. With Icolyn continuing in domestic service it wasn't long before she was able to move from living in a single room in French Street to Eric's two-bedroom flat at 28, Blunt Street. Although life was undoubtedly difficult, Eric and Icolyn were industrious and worked hard – and they had to, because Norman soon had a brother, George.

Fortunately, they were able to buy a two-bedroom bungalow in Trench Town, 11 Farham Road, in a new development in Waterhouse, and there the two boys were joined by two sisters, christened Pamela and Paulette. Eric, who was hoping for more sons, melted when he saw them. Holding baby Pamela in his hands for the first time, he lovingly likened her to the delicacy of blossom, and Blossom has become the name by which she is generally known. The birth of Paulette again inspired poetry in him, describing her as a beautiful dawn, so Dawn is the name that most people use. Icolyn gave up full-time work but to supplement the family income she bought bales of cotton off-cuts which she turned into clothes, curtains and bed linen and sold from a market stall.

This was a much healthier environment in which to raise a family; the bungalow had a garden big enough for chickens, pigs and goats, as well as an area fenced off for growing vegetables. Sometimes Eric got up early to cycle to the nearby seashore to catch fish before starting the day's work. They also had two dogs and two donkeys – Spider and Doris, and two goats – King and Queen, which were tethered in waste land and fed themselves. School was over a mile walk away; the boys had to return home for lunch so they had a lot of walking to do, every day. Although the discipline at school was strict and money was obviously tight, the children were oblivious to hardship and deprivation.

Although Icolyn remembers life in Kingston with pleasure it must have been difficult – and dangerous. Jones Town, where she first went to live with Mary was a run-down, lawless neighbourhood. Through it ran Spanish Town Road, formerly a thriving centre for commerce and entertainment but, in the 1950s, well into its long decline. And although Icolyn was attracted to its bright lights and dance halls, it was for good reason that she would never go alone. On the other side of the Spanish Town Road was Back-o-Wall, little more than a slum and one of the areas over which Jamaica's emerging political parties fought for votes with bribery and, if necessary, violence.

Back-o-Wall's fearsome reputation was already known in Icolyn's school, back in Gubay. A young lad had come from there and his aggressive, urban background had made him a bully. One day he got into a fight and lost, and his father came to complain to the head teacher. When the father realised who his son had been fighting, he left without another word being said. That person was Icolyn.

Despite life's difficulties there was usually something to celebrate. One such occasion took place in November 1953. when the newly-crowned Queen Elizabeth, and her husband Prince Philip, came on an official visit. The crowds were immense and Icolyn, being so short, saw nothing of the royal party. However she remembers the policemen, looking so smart in their black trousers and caps, white tunics and red sashes. It was a bank holiday; there was music and dancing everywhere and the island's newspaper, *The Gleaner*, enjoyed its biggest sales ever.

Jamaican politics had been polarised from the first stirrings of pre-War independence by the Jamaican Labour Party and the People's National Party, formed by very different men who were, in

Cousins but political rivals: Alexander Bustamante and Norman Manley

fact, cousins. One was Alexander Bustamente, a huge man, wildly extrovert with a gift for oratory. He made himself champion of the poor and dispossessed and urged them to fight against colonial servitude. His cousin, Norman Washington Manley, was a brilliant but rather academic lawyer; he formed the People's National Party, based on Britain's Labour Party, and advocated extensive public ownership and social welfare. To begin with, these seemingly compatible ideologies worked together to discourage unrest and the promise of reform. As a result, Jamaica became the first British colony to be granted full adult suffrage. However, in the run-up to Jamaica's first election in 1944, differences emerged, with Bustamente's Jamaican Labour Party representing conservative interests and Manley's People's National Party maintaining its radical position. As time went on, these differences tended to be about power and money, and less about ideology.

For those, like Icolyn and Eric, who lived in Kingston's urban areas, there was no escaping what passed for politics at the time. Groups of men canvassed households about their voting intentions and a wrong answer could result in intimidation. Neither Icolyn nor Eric had any political interest but if they had been marked out as supporting one party or another, there would be people who would shout at them in the street and outside their house. Rallies and political meetings became dangerous affairs and they stayed away.

These tensions worsened as Jamaica moved towards independence. But Icolyn remembers Independence Day, 6 August 1962, as a day of joy and celebration in which all the old rivalries and bitterness were mysteriously forgotten. The carnival atmosphere went on for days and the national colours of green, yellow and black were seen everywhere – on flags, clothes and hoardings. At last, Jamaica began to feel good about itself and although its problems did not go away, Icolyn believes this feel-good factor persisted for the rest of the time she was there.

A contributory factor towards the goodwill of the day was the visit of Princess Margaret as the Queen's official representative. Paradoxically, independence did little to undermine the huge respect and affection in which most people held the Royal Family. Indeed Icolyn remembers the occasion of a special broadcast to Jamaica by King George VI in 1944. Everyone who could, clustered around their radios, listening to the royal message in reverential silence.

As Jamaica's traditional dependence on Britain waned, and despite increasing investment and political influence from the United States, the economy suffered along with the prospects of those struggling with poverty in Kingston's shantytowns. But people recognised that life was for living and far from being indolent, they were active: Icolyn remembers that the day began as dawn broke, with people running for exercise. It was a habit that was celebrated half a century later at the 2012 Olympics with a gold medal for the 100m sprint won by Usain Bolt, who is widely regarded as the fastest man ever. It was also an era which saw the beginning of Jamaica's great surge onto the world's music scene and for those who had little else, life was sustained by the joy inspired by song and dance.

All day and throughout the night, Kingston throbbed to the sound of music played on home-made instruments and recorded on 12-inch and 7-inch vinyl discs. It was constant and often so close and loud that sleep was impossible but, like the underlying menace that still prevailed, Icolyn says 'you just got used to it.' Jamaicans have music-making in them from the toe-nails upwards. Even those who had little else used considerable ingenuity in stretching skins over various containers to make drums, or crafting a guitar out of bamboo growing on the roadside, its strings made from sisal. Few had any musical training but that presented no barrier to the excitement and creativity generated by those instinctive performers.

Music was, however, like much in Jamaican society, a male-dominated preserve and the closest Icolyn got to any involvement was through a friend who knew Slim & Sam. They were street singers who published a new song every week, their lyrics based on current events and notorious individuals. Their reflections of the times attracted huge attention but those who bought the song-sheets saw only the words; Icolyn, through her friend's introduction, heard the tunes too.

Probably, more than anyone else, it was Bob Marley who introduced the world to reggae. Reggae has its origins in traditional African music, influenced by American jazz and blues, fused in the back streets of Kingston into ska. This distinctive sound emphasises the off-beat, known as the skank, usually played on guitar and a term which effectively describes the sound it makes. Other complex rhythms and melodies weave around this frame and it is in its later developments, played at a slower tempo, that it became known as reggae. While other forms of popular music are often based on romance, reggae makes frequent use of lyrics for social comment, sometimes with reference to the use of ganga, or cannabis. It also became associated with Rastafaris.

And with his dreadlocks, it was Bob Marley who made the wider world aware of Rastafaris. This spiritual movement of Jamaican origin arose around the time of Icolyn's birth with the socio-political, black nationalist manifesto of Marcus Garvey. Although its followers regard it more as a way of life than a religion, Rastafari is based very much on a particular interpretation of the Old Testament, and a belief that Emperor Haile Sellasie of Ethiopia, who died in 1974, was Christ in His second appearance on Earth. Politically, Rastafaris espouse repatriation to Africa, which they call Zion, social equality among all peoples and a rejection of western values, which they refer to as Babylon. The symbolic wearing of dreadlocks is directed, they believe, by Leviticus 21.5 and Numbers 6.5 while verses from Genesis, Psalms, Proverbs and Revelation are taken to endorse the sacramental use of ganga. In contrast to the sometimes threatening atmosphere in the Kingston shanties, the Rastafarians, always small in number, represent a dreamy, gentle idealism and unattainable goals. Icolyn often passed a group of them, spending their days sitting around and smoking, a veil of dreadlocks completely obscuring their faces. Many found their sinister appearance and mysterious beliefs intimidating, but Icolyn drew them into conversation and they would hail her as 'Sister.'

As far as Icolyn was concerned the Rastafaris were just harmless members of the community, but she was surprised one day when a dreadlocked neighbour knocked on her door and said 'Sister – I was just passing and felt like giving you this,' and he handed her a threepenny piece. Then he drifted on his way, afloat on ganga. Icolyn believes his visit was a helping hand from God, because she had three hungry children in the house, and no food. On another occasion a Rasta gave her a bunch of dried ganga stalks 'for her baby' who, he had heard, was unwell. He told her to add them to boiling water for a tea and, when it was cool, to give it to the baby. She did so, and the baby began to recover. Ganga was like a weed, growing on roadsides and uncultivated ground everywhere, Icolyn recalls. Thirty years later, her youngest son Gary, by then a special constable, revealed to her that ganga was cannabis. In Jamaica it was so common that it had no value, unlike that more dangerous drug which came to fuel much of Jamaican crime – cocaine.

Norman Manley complained that Jamaicans had to wait so long for independence that when they finally got it, they didn't know what to do with it. The lawlessness which accompanied political life since Jamaicans got the vote only grew worse after independence, and the accompanying violence was never far below the surface. In 1966 Icolyn's brother Colin, who worked in Kingston as a barber, was attacked on his way home from Spanish Town for no obvious reason, and died later of stab wounds. Within a couple of years, Hedley was dead too – shot through his car window. His associates caught the assassin, an off-duty policeman, and he was himself shot. Although the identity of both murderers was known, that is where justice ended; neither case came to trial. Hedley had come to Kingston to work as a carpenter and he had succeeded in establishing a business as a government contractor; he employed people and owned a nice car and the other rewards of hard work. Success was a dangerous thing in post-independence Jamaica and it seems likely that he had been sucked into a vicious circle of envy and extortion; what is more certain is that he had earned himself the nickname 'Money Brown' and, inevitably, enemies. The shock of this incident drew the family together and Icolyn flew out from the UK to help comfort her elderly parents, still living in Coolshade.

4

A Grey, Unpleasant land

Although the children were happy growing up in Kingston, Icolyn and Eric were concerned about the future. Work was becoming increasingly difficult to find and, in 1960 it was decided that Eric should do what so many of his fellow countrymen had done, and take the boat for England. His sister was already settled in this country and, later, Icolyn's sister Martha and brother Seymour were to make the same journey. It must have been a very difficult decision to divide the family, leaving Icolyn to bring up Norman, George,

The early days of AERE Harwell

Blossom and Dawn on her own. To make ends meet, she took up work in a factory making shirts from Jamaican cotton for export to the US. For many, such a five-year separation would become unsustainable but she and Eric wrote to each other every two weeks and worked hard, determined that the family should be united again as soon as possible. Fortunately Icolyn was strong-willed and self-confident and confronted life's difficulties with a simple determination to get on with it, an attitude which must have seen her through some dark and difficult times. Eric's regular remittances from England eased some of the financial pressures of bringing up four children.

For Eric the long voyage across the cold, grey Atlantic, arriving eventually in cold, grey London must have been a daunting experience. Britain was still recovering from the devastation of war and had little concern for its growing population of immigrants, but that recovery meant work and Eric had little difficulty in finding employment almost immediately. He was able to stay with his sister in London until he got settled. He then responded to a call for skilled workers to help build the new Atomic Energy Research Establishment at Harwell, at the foot of the Berkshire Downs and not far from Oxford. He found accommodation in Chiswell Road, off the Abingdon Road in south Oxford.

Harwell had been in a state of rapid development almost since the end of the War and its first reactors and laboratories had been completed by the time Eric arrived. Harwell was a former RAF airfield which had been very active in the Normandy landings and on later bombing raids over Germany; the site was therefore already well-supplied with buildings which simply needed conversion. The big need, however, was for housing. Several hundred prefabs were built at Harwell itself to be replaced eventually by more conventional housing, and entire housing estates owned by the Authority, were built in Abingdon, Grove and Newbury. Harwell soon outgrew its original location and additional facilities were built at nearly Culham, the site of another redundant air base, formerly used as a training centre for aircraft flown by the Royal Navy. It is probable that Eric worked on many of these sites, reaching them in the fleet of special buses which the Authority provided for transporting its employees to work, and sometimes in a van owned by one of his colleagues.

*Icolyn with Norman, George, Blossom
and Dawn before leaving for England*

At the beginning of 1965 it was decided that the family could, at last, afford the £85 one-way ticket for Icolyn to rejoin Eric in the UK. The children were sent up to Coolshade to live with their grandparents and, after promising to send for them when she was settled in England, Icolyn boarded a BOAC Britannia for the long, cramped, noisy flight to London. She was met at Heathrow by Eric and her first impressions of the mother country were far from favourable; it was cold and inhospitable but Eric convinced her that she would get used to it. In Oxford, she was shocked to see so many houses with smoke pouring from their chimneys and thought they were factories. Undeterred though, she immediately adapted to her new life; she arrived on a Friday and began her first job on the following Monday. It was in the canteen of the Morris car factory in Cowley, run by the catering company Peter Merchant, where she worked in all roles from serving to washing up. The motor industry was one of the UK's driving forces in the economic boom of the 1960s, much of it centred on Cowley; jobs there were highly prized and well paid, and even though she was not on the shop floor herself, Icolyn was often earning more than Eric.

When Icolyn arrived she and Eric rented a room in Magdalen Road for three months before securing a mortgage to buy 35 Randolph Street which was to be their home for the next 21 years. It had three bedrooms and during the next five months they got it ready for the children, and managed to save up enough for their air fares.

For Norman, George, Blossom and Dawn, the journey must have been a harrowing experience. Knowing only the tropical climate of Jamaica, winter weather caused their flight to be diverted first to New York and then to Manchester; and when they finally arrived at Heathrow, they were greeted by blizzards. More than the fear and uncertainty of change, their main memory is of being so cold. But they were not alone; there were many more unaccompanied children on their flight, rejoining parents who had already emigrated, and they were cared for by specially trained air crew. Icolyn and Eric had been waiting for the long-delayed flight, a wait which must have been anxious and uncomfortable in the terminal's rudimentary facilities. But the family was reunited. The children were bundled into coats, clothing with which they were totally unfamiliar; by the time they reached Oxford it was dark and the children had been travelling for 24 hours. Norman was 14, George, 13, Blossom 11 and Dawn just 8.

Their first impressions of their new home were not good. In Jamaica the only houses with chimneys were bakeries; the house in

Randolph Street had chimneys and they did not want to live in a bakery. But they didn't have a choice of course, and the house which must have seemed rather empty before, was now full. It was very well positioned for a growing family in Oxford in the 1960s. Within a few minutes' walk there were the schools, which educated them all, the College of Further Education and the Co-op. On the other side of Cowley Road was a small park, and central Oxford was easily reached by bus. Looking back now, all four of those children who made the journey from Jamaica reckon it took five years for them to adjust to their new life; in fact the family always had a hope that they might eventually return to Jamaica, a hope which always seemed to be five years in the future. Through their eyes, Jamaica was a paradise which, as time went on, became increasingly unattainable.

Soon after he joined East Oxford Secondary School Norman asked his mother if he could bring a schoolfriend home for lunch. This was Hilroy Burton, the same age and an immigrant too, from Antigua. Things were unsettled in his own home and lunch at Randolph Street became more frequent; eventually he actually moved in, becoming a member of a family into which he integrated easily. Within a year Icolyn found she was expecting another baby; this was Gary, who she always calls 'the little lad' but who grew up to be by far the biggest of them all. By then the three-bedroom house in Randolph Street was accommodating two adults, three boys, two girls and a baby, and Eric set about extending it and modernising it.

One day Icolyn passed a house in Hawkins Street and noticed some children peering anxiously through the window. She knocked on the door and a small voice called through the letterbox that their mother had told them not to open the door to strangers. She asked if they were hungry and they were, so she returned with some cake. This time the door was opened and she was appalled by what she saw. The house was damp and very unhealthy for small children; there was also very little furniture in it. Without hesitation, Icolyn took the children to her own home and, later, collected their mother too. There they stayed for several weeks while they looked for a better place of their own. This spirit of generosity housed several other people over the years and, though instinctive to Icolyn, was typical of immigrant families, who often offered shelter to their fellows until they got settled. But in that household, shelter was extended to anyone in need – of any race or background. So however much Eric extended the house, it was always full. And so was the cooking pot. However many people were in the house at the time, Icolyn always cooked for more, just in case someone should arrive who needed feeding, as often they did.

Randolph Street has terraced Victorian housing, opening straight onto the pavement but few of the houses had the conveniences we now take for granted; Number 35 was heated by paraffin stoves which produced a lot of condensation and were a real hazard with young children running about. Money was always tight and, like so many housewives, Icolyn grew to depend on the Co-operative Wholesale Society whose dividends and credit arrangements for regular savers enabled her to buy essentials for the family and, particularly, school clothes. She often had to assert her forceful personality in order to maintain discipline and it was Eric who decided that, within the family, she should be called by her maiden name, Miss Brown. The name stuck and that is how the family addresses her still, nearly 50 years later. When the three eldest boys, Norman, George and Hilroy left school and began earning a wage, it was Icolyn's discipline which made sure they each contributed regularly to a fund which was used exclusively for the deposit on a house for each of them. And this 'partner' scheme, as it is called, still continues, with Icolyn taking care of the cash.

Almost as soon as the family settled in Oxford they had to confront the seamier side of life in Britain – discrimination; they faced it in shops, in the workplace and at the children's schools. Even the teachers were, as Icolyn recalls, 'not very pleasant'. Once she snatched a little boy from the path of a car in Cowley Road only to be told by his mother to 'take your black hands off my boy'. She refused to let this kind of behaviour intimidate her but Eric, of a more sensitive nature, had his confidence undermined. Icolyn was stoical about it: history showed how much the British had taken from her country, and as far as Icolyn was concerned, she and her fellow Jamaicans were now going to take some of it back. Although she would normally take abuse unflinchingly, it was a different matter when it came to the children. A racial altercation in the local launderette resulted in Dawn being hit by the manageress; Eric saw it as his duty to attempt a reconciliation but Icolyn had no patience for that. While Eric was still nervously negotiating in the launderette, she marched in, hit the manageress fair and square, and marched out again. It seems to have solved the problem.

Discrimination was a shock to her children who kept asking the question 'Why?', a question which remains unanswered. In Jamaica they had lived in a multi-racial community which certainly made judgements on their fellows, but never on the basis of the colour of their skin, despite the presence of paler complexions as a reminder of their tragic history. George reflected that back in Kingston his best friends had been Albert and Vincent Hoo, twins born of Chinese parents but speaking the Jamaican patois. He had inherited his mother's fighting spirit though, and was often involved in scraps which earned him respect at school. Later, discrimination became a serious problem for Norman. When he left school he was taken on as an apprentice electrician by local contractors, Ilco. Under this arrangement he was supposed to be given a day off a week to attend the College of Further Education, but he was kept working. The white apprentices went to college and got their qualification, but Norman did not.

5

Making the Best of It

In the 1960s, daily life in Cowley Road was characterised by the flow of hundreds of bicycles on their way to the morning shift in the Cowley car factories and, in the opposite direction at the end of

The tidal wave of bicycles in Cowley Road in the 1960s.
Courtesy of Oxford Mail/The Oxford Times
(Newsquest Oxfordshire)

day as their owners returned home. When times were good there was a night shift too. For residents in the neighbouring streets, this regular, passing traffic helped support a wide variety of shops, pubs and health services. It was even said 'There is no need to go into town; everything can be got on the Cowley Road'.

But Britain was still struggling to rebuild the country's resources lost in the War and to adjust to an economy based partly on a diminishing empire. The pound was devalued and attempts to find security in membership of the European Economic Community were rebuffed. In 1973 the Middle-east oil-producing nations imposed an embargo on supplies as part of a wider conflict, and the price of crude oil quadrupled overnight. Industrial action by coal-miners led to the imposition of a three-day working week in order to conserve energy. In the meantime the country's economic position worsened, aggravated by widespread strike action.

In Oxford, car production was drastically affected by a growing militancy among the workforce and a weak, authoritarian manage-ment resulted in strikes and mass pickets. There must have been times when Icolyn and Eric wondered if, in leaving the troubles of Jamaica, they had only found new ones in Britain.

After Gary was born Icolyn gave up the job in the Peter Merchant canteen to become a full-time mother. In addition to the baby she had five other growing children to look after and, although the household budget was tight, Eric was earning good money and the family just about managed. But then, in 1970, he had a stroke, the first of many. It happened while he was on some scaffolding but, fortunately, his work mates managed to get him down safely. He recovered without much lasting damage but, on Christmas morning, Icolyn saw Eric looking at himself strangely in the mirror. The left side of his face was drawn and his speech was slurred. She recognised the symptoms of another stroke and called the family GP, Dr Lawrence, who came immediately. He sent for an ambulance and Eric was taken to the Radcliffe Infirmary in Woodstock Road. That stroke was worse than the rest and although he could walk, he was no longer fit enough for the tough outdoor life of a carpenter on building sites. Eventually he found work as a kitchen porter in the new John Radcliffe Hospital and, later, in the Slade Hospital, but at wages far below those necessary to feed a family of eight.

Icolyn had to return to work. Work was something she had always been used to and she was not one for staying at home all day. And work of the very kind for which she was best suited was close at hand: Cowley Road Hospital, just across the road from Randolph Street. This venerable institution, of striking architecture and now sadly demolished, was known locally as the Workhouse, which indeed it had been, but not for 50 years. As a hospital, it was then used primarily to treat geriatric and stroke patients, and Icolyn applied to become a nurse.

Life was simpler in those days. There was no talk of qualifications; aptitude and common sense were all that were required and she

Cowley Road Hospital. Courtesy of Oxford Mail/The Oxford Times (Newsquest Oxfordshire)

clearly had those in abundance. At her interview with a certain Staff
Nurse Honeywell she made it clear that her family came first so
there would be no night-shifts, and that if she was needed at home,
she would have to go there. Without any more formalities she was
measured up for her uniform, and started work on the following
Monday. She worked 42 hours a week, including alternate weekends,
for £30 a month, paid in cash.

Under the watchful eye of Staff Nurse Honeywell Icolyn did just
one week of theoretical training. She learned about the care of
patients, how to lift them and how to make beds. On the job she
learned the essential skills of hygiene, how to wash patients and how
to help them regain their self-respect, as often they had become
disfigured by their illness. Her cheerful banter encouraged them; she
brushed their hair and helped women with their makeup; sometimes
she gave them a hug. Although the hospital had its own cleaning
staff she made it her special responsibility to make sure that the
sluice room was always spotless.

Those were good days and she has many happy memories from
the three years she worked there. Much of that happiness was due to
the appreciation shown by her patients, many of whom were stricken
by age and infirmity but who managed to preserve their dignity and
sense of humour. Fragmentary memories drift by, such as the farmer
from Bampton who, though severely ill, asked his wife to bring in
gifts for the staff. She was very small, Icolyn remembers – smaller
even than she was herself; unlike the very large woman who, before
her illness had helped build up the family business of Durham's, one
of Oxford's greengrocers, from its early beginnings selling door-to-
door on a handcart, to its city-centre shops supplying the Colleges.
Or the hospital porter who placed bets at the bookies for one of the
patients, and who passed on a special tip to all the staff. It was for
Red Rum, an outstanding racehorse of the day, and Icolyn's luck was
in. Her threepenny bet won her two shillings.

Some of her patients, however, were not so appreciative and old
prejudices surfaced again. Once, a patient in a side room hit out at
her because of her colour, and another, an educated and sophisticated

man from the Curry family which began the chain of electrical shops and who was recovering from a stroke, kicked her with his good leg and told her not to touch him. Naturally she felt angered and humiliated by such experiences but she was always supported by her stern, no-nonsense matron, Sister Fitzgerald, who knew how to deal with troublesome patients. In any case, through the contrasting phases of her life beginning in rural Jamaica to the tensions of Kingston and her displacement to a very different land thousands of miles away, Icoloyn had learned a lot about human nature. It was a fear of the unknown, she concluded, which made people turn on minorities and it was this simple understanding which enabled her to continue providing this same care, even to Mr Curry. And, in the end, even he treated her with the respect she deserved.

She has happy memories, too, of her colleagues, and she is still in touch with some of them, over forty years later. Amid gales of laughter she tells of Dr Wilmer – 'a lovely person' – who was constantly losing her glasses. On one of her ward rounds, while sitting on a patient's bed, she absently removed the glasses from the patient's face and put them on her own.

It was during this time that Icolyn acquired an injury from which she still suffers. While lifting a patient she suddenly felt – and heard – a crack in her wrist, followed by excruciating pain. The matter was duly noted in the Accident Book but it put severe limitations on what she could do, a serious problem because she was by now the main bread-winner in the household. Two weeks later an X-ray revealed that a bone had been broken and an operation at the Nuffield Orthopaedic Centre left her arm, from elbow to hand, encased in plaster. But after two more weeks the pain was no better, and she was bleeding, indicating the presence of an infection, which could have necessitated amputation. She was referred to a specialist in Banbury who immediately realised that her treatment at the Nuffield was inappropriate but he could do nothing about it, he told her, because 'doctors don't go against doctors'. This was a disgraceful episode but, in the end, nature began the healing process on its own.

Icolyn worked at Cowley Road Hospital until tragedy struck in the family and her caring skills were needed at home. In the summer of 1975 Eric became seriously ill and Dr Lawrence once again referred him to the Radcliffe Infirmary. This time he was found to have a malignant tumour, and investigations showed that it had progressed too far for an operation to be successful. The consultant did not know how to break the news to Icolyn and was unable to look her in the eye as he skirted round the subject; he did not know that despite her size, she was a very strong person and familiar with serious illness through her work at Cowley Road Hospital. To his considerable relief, it was she who first used the dreaded word cancer. Despite protests from healthcare professionals that she would be unable to manage, Icolyn took him back to Randolph Street and nursed him to the end. There was nothing else to be done, she decided, and he had a right to die in his own bed. It took nine months for the end to come and although Eric did not have to endure much pain, he suffered terribly from the side effects of chemotherapy, a treatment which, in those days was still in its infancy. Dr Lawrence visited him every day and offered Icolyn sleeping pills, which she declined. She believed it was her newly-discovered faith that kept her going: 'What is to be, is to be' she believed; in the end, reconciled to the inevitable, she declared 'Lord – this is your part, not mine. You know I can't do this, but you can.' As the end seemed close, a distraught Icolyn whispered to Eric 'We all make mistakes with each other – please forgive me.' Eric whispered back 'I made a lot of mistakes too – do you forgive me?' He died the following day, 3 March 1976, in his bed at home and surrounded by his family, as both of them had intended. In the days that followed some of the pain of grief was swept away in the traditional Jamaica celebrations to mark Eric's passing and the house was full of visitors and friends, eating, drinking and singing.

Although nine-year old Gary understood that something awful was happening, he did not take in the full enormity of his father's death, and raced back to school. In the Jamaican tradition, Norman now stepped into the role as head of the family to support his

*Eric Smith, husband to Icolyn and father of
Norman, George, Blossom, Dawn and Gary*

mother and his younger brothers and sisters. There was, of course, much to be done of a practical as well as emotional nature, and not much time in which to do it, because he was due to get married just three weeks later. This was in itself a reminder of Eric's death because his suit had been remodelled to fit his shrunken body in the hope that he might survive to see the wedding. On top of all that, Icolyn herself was unwell; she had fibroids, a very painful condition. Nevertheless she busied herself with wedding preparations, including making the cake, and when it was over, she had to go to hospital. Dr Lawrence told her that she was 'As tough as old boots,' to which Icolyn exclaimed 'What a thing to say!'

Then George was married three months after Norman. Even Icolyn's strength and resilience must have been put to the test in coping with so many life-changing events in such a short time. But, she remembers with a smile, Norman was so much help and to make sure his youngest brother realised he was not forgotten, he bought nine-year old Gary a 'chopper', a small-wheeled bicycle with a back-rest, which was the height of fashion at the time. It was a demonstration of family ties, derived from their Jamaican roots, which has persisted into the generations to follow. Unlike so many families which are disconnected and dispersed in Britain today, Icolyn feels that her sons and daughters, their wives and husbands, together with her grandchildren are just one big, caring family

And caring had become Icolyn's vocation. When she felt able to return to work it was with the Social Services, helping people unable to cope with the turmoil in their lives. In this she saw humanity at its most desperate, whether it was single mothers with unruly children, elderly people too incapacitated even to get themselves into bed, those suffering from the shock of bereavement or families that had been broken by financial difficulties, crime, violence or drink.

6

From Cowley Road to Coolshade

Like most immigrants, Icolyn assumed that she and the family would, one day, return to the country of their birth. Secretly, she had been saving for this eventuality from the moment she started working in the Peter Merchant canteen in the car factory. Her return, but not for the reason she expected, or so soon or so urgently, came within three years, following the horrible death of her brother, Hedley. Fortunately, she had managed to save nearly all the £160 required for her air fare.

Four years later she was summoned again. One day in 1972, while Icolyn was working at the back of the house in Randolph Street, a knock on the front door was answered by Blossom. It was a telegram from Jamaica and obviously important, so important that she felt the need to consult her oldest brother, Norman, about what to do with it. But Normans wasn't there, so it was not until he came back from work that he could take charge and give the telegram to Icolyn. It contained the news that her father had died.

Icolyn managed to get a flight out just two days later; her ticket offered free flights for children so she took Gary with her. After an exhausting journey they were met at the airport and driven to Gubay, still a mile from Coolshade but the road went no nearer. There she found the rest of the family waiting for her, waiting indeed for Icolyn to decide what should be done; in the meantime her father's body was in the undertakers in Kingston.

News of Icolyn's arrival from the UK spread quickly around the neighbourhood, in the same way that people heard about George's death very soon after it happened. Someone called out into the evening; others heard the message and called it out themselves. In this way anything newsworthy in rural Jamaica rippled from the villages into the fields and out into the hills within minutes. And in this way, everyone heard that the funeral was to be held in two days' time.

There was no specific time because funerals in Jamaica are all-day affairs. They are a celebration of the deceased's passing and, like every other celebration, involve much singing and dancing, eating and drinking. There was a period of solemnity in the late afternoon when the local minister arrived to say a few words but it was only brief because George was not a church-goer; then the party resumed and continued into the night. And that was just the beginning.

Although she was now a widow, it was many weeks before Nelly was alone. It is a belief throughout the Caribbean that the pain of grief can be dissipated if it can be shared, so no-one is left to grieve on their own. Nelly's home was therefore full; people would arrive uninvited and say 'I'm staying tonight', and they did. In the meantime her neighbours looked after George's crops and livestock, and ensured that Nelly always had all the food and provisions she needed. In the tradition of the Caribbean, the community looked after her.

In fact, Nelly was never entirely alone. Years earlier, as her children were leaving the family to strike out on their own, 17-year old Seymour had made a local girl pregnant. It was a secret he kept sheepishly to himself, taking care to maintain his distance from the girl and his daughter. Soon after the birth, the baby's mother proved incapable of looking after her and she was handed over to an aunt, who was blind as well as old, and who could manage little better. In the meantime, Seymour's secret had been revealed because the little baby looked exactly like him, and she was brought to Nelly. So, well into middle age, George and Nelly found themselves responsible for a malnourished, nine-month old little girl, who they brought up as their own daughter. This was Dorrett, who was just a teenager when George died, and who continued to live with Nelly for a further thirteen years.

Icolyn had already considered Oxford to be her home but she received such a welcome on visiting Coolshade that she felt a distinct pull to stay in Jamaica. She spent the week following the funeral looking after her mother and reuniting with her remaining family and friends. There was much to tell of her new life in Oxford, and much to hear about events in Coolshade, and the week passed quickly. She and Gary spent a night in Kingston with more friends before flying home.

For Gary the whole experience was overwhelming. He was the only one of the family to be born outside Jamaica and was a product of 20th century British consumerism. As far as he was concerned, oranges and bananas came from supermarkets, not from trees and he was only persuaded to eat them after a pretence was made that they had been bought from a shop. Their night in Kingston coincided with Gary's birthday but he was in no mood to celebrate. Only when they were back in the familiar surroundings of their home in Oxford, and the event was marked in proper style, did he then believe that he was six years old.

Then, in June 1985, another telegram arrived; this time about Nelly. Icolyn flew to Jamaica on her own; she was met at the airport and taken straight to Coolshade. Once again her extended family was awaiting her arrival and, once again, no decisions had been made about what was to be done. There was a poignancy to the celebrations this time because Nelly was the last of the family to live in Coolshade. As a particular mark of respect the undertaker dressed Nelly in a beautiful, lace white gown that Icolyn had brought over from England. The following day the house was empty; Dorrett had left the village for America some time earlier, and Icolyn spent two weeks in Kingston with her sisters, Vi and Enid, before flying home.

Despite the pleasure in meeting family and friends again, it was a long two weeks and, in contrast to the time of her father's funeral, Icolyn felt homesick for her husband, children and her life in Oxford. In any case, Jamaica was changing and she did not feel part of it. Some things were better – the roads, for example, but much else seemed to be neglected. The market where, years earlier, she had a stall to sell the clothes she made at home was still functioning, just, but it had become badly run down. Jamaica was still struggling to make its way in the world.

That generation may have passed but it is not forgotten. There is a family burial plot in Coolshade and in it there are the graves of George and Nelly, their sons Colin and Hedley who met violent deaths in Kingston, and Icolyn's eldest brother, Arnold.

Years later there was another call from Jamaica, this time by telephone and from the parish of St Mary's. It was to tell of the death of Icolyn's sister, Vi, and in accordance with custom, the call went to the oldest remaining member of the family, Martha. Martha had also emigrated to England and was living in Long Eaton in Nottinghamshire. She was an elderly lady herself and in some confusion about what to do, but Icolyn had no doubt. She bought two tickets for a flight leaving Manchester the next day and Martha agreed to join her for their sister's funeral. Sadly, the experience traumatised Martha, somehow causing her to stop eating. Despite medication and hospital care, it wasn't long before she, too, had died.

After Vi's death, Enid and Mandley were the only members of Icolyn's immediate family still to be living in Jamaica. Many of the next generation remain, of course, and relatives now occupy the house in which Icolyn and Eric brought up four children before the move to Oxford. It is probable that the family farms in Coolshade have been neglected and, without cultivation, have been engulfed by Jamaica's rapacious natural vegetation.

Jamaica has since become a popular holiday destination for every member of the family and they have returned many times. Although they now regard their home to be in England Dawn, in particular, still feels the pull of her Jamaican roots.

7

The Next 24 Years

'Hello Mrs Smith!' It was a familiar greeting down Cowley Road. But Icolyn struggled to place this tall, smiling young man. He was of Asian appearance and in his late twenties. Seeing her discomfort he laughed 'You were my Nanny.' Then it all came back to her. This was Iqbal, the oldest of three children whose mother had injured herself in a fall, and was unable to cope. Their father was working all hours and was never there when he was needed; in any case Pakistani men were culturally unprepared for bringing up children. A desperate situation was rescued by the Social Services and, for several weeks the family became Icolyn's clients. Icolyn's main recollection is of the youngest in the family, a squirming, squealing little baby, so it was hardly surprising that she didn't recognise Iqbal now. 'Would you like to come to my wedding?' he asked, half jokingly. It was to be in Pakistan and Iqbal had yet to meet his bride.

Weddings, christenings, funerals: Icolyn had been invited to so many by people who had passed through her life but, of course, she could not go to this one. For over forty years, from her time as a nurse in Cowley Road Hospital to her vocation in the Soup Kitchen, her instinctive compassion for anyone in need had provided a lifeline which they rarely forgot. After Eric's death in 1976 she was left with young Gary and two teenage daughters to bring up on her own and financial pressures must have been considerable. Looking back on the difficulties of that period and how she got through it, Gary's wife Yvonne says 'That was God'.

What she needed was a morning job which began after she had taken Gary to school, and left her with enough time to do the cooking, clean the house and collect Gary in the afternoon. It was her niece, Monica, who telephoned to suggest she should try the Social Services. At the City Chambers, where the Social Services offices were at the time, her application to become a home help for young families in need, the elderly and the disabled, was accepted immediately; she had excellent references and they could accommodate her reduced hours. She was also so used to dealing with infirm patients, who were often difficult or incontinent, that she was given just one week's training, assisting a more experienced colleague on her rounds, and then she was on her own.

Throughout her time with the Service Icolyn helped her elderly clients out of bed, washed them, fed them, made sure they were taking their medication and that their domestic arrangements were satisfactory; if necessary she would also do their cleaning and shopping. They were of all ages and both sexes and some, like Bishop George Appleton (the subject of a separate chapter) were from Oxford's academic sector. She provided emotional support and constant good humour, despite the distressing conditions she sometimes encountered in her work. Her attitude to clients who could not look after themselves was that they deserved the same care as anyone else, and she was determined to provide it. Some, like Iqbal, were deeply appreciative, but others resented their disabilities, indignities and, often, sheer loneliness. Icolyn earned a reputation for calming stress and dealing decisively with whatever problems she found. Fearlessly, she demanded medical help when it was clearly needed though sometimes it came too late; she became used to dealing with death.

When Gary was old enough to look after himself she took on an evening shift as well so that she could provide her clients with continuity throughout the day. Her rota was posted to her weekly by her supervisor, Elizabeth Richardson, and she could find herself visiting homes anywhere between Marston, Cowley, Blackbird Leys and Iffley Road; she did not have a car and never mastered a bicycle so she got there by bus and by walking.

Icolyn does not look back on this 24-year period of her life with much satisfaction because the vital work which she and her

The family home in Randolph Street

colleagues were undertaking seemed so undervalued by their employers. She enjoyed the work and built up strong relationships with her clients who often came to depend on her, but she was capable of so much more, a capability which was to be fulfilled towards the end of her career with the Social Services. In the meantime she moved house.

The Randolph Street home was much bigger on the inside than it appears from the street and it has a large garden. With the extension that Eric had built it was ideal for a large family, even one which often had to accommodate others who found themselves in housing difficulties. However, all this was to change in the few months covered by Eric's death and the marriages of Norman and George; Dawn and Hilroy had already moved away and suddenly Icolyn, Blossom and Gary were left on their own. Besides, it was an old house which cost a lot to heat and maintain.

So in 1988 Icolyn decided to look for somewhere smaller, anticipating the time when Blossom and Gary might want their independence; she also had to consider the prospect of living on her own – something she had never done in her life before. Once the decision had been made the wide choice of new homes was narrowed to those close to a bus route and the area she already knew, and this led to 4 Kelburne Road.

The move was achieved in a day; Norman hired a van and every member of the family became furniture removers. But moving from a large house to a smaller one always presents problems and there was simply no room for everything, so much of it had to go. Icolyn's first reaction to her new home was one of misgiving; she felt she was leaving Eric and the family's spirit behind, and she feared no-one would find her among the similar-looking streets of Littlemore. It was only a temporary feeling however; she soon got to work modernising the house and adding a new extension, and she had Blossom for company for several more years.

Meanwhile, Icolyn's true vocation was beginning to emerge. It was the role of the Social Services to come to the aid of the distressed in their homes but what about those who had no home? The problem was all too obvious, particularly around Cowley Road Hospital. The only agency that seemed to be responsible was the police, who only became involved when individuals became troublesome. For the first few years of the Soup Kitchen she tried to combine it with her work as a home help but that soon became impossible so she asked Mrs Richardson if she could have Wednesdays off. Permission was granted but on the understanding that she would make up the time on another day.

4 Kelburne Road, Littlemore

This is a sad reflection on the Social Services at the time; the management seemed unconcerned about the welfare of its own staff and moral was as low as the wages. Icolyn was already well past retiring age and in nearly 24 years service she had never taken a day off through illness. When she finally decided to retire, she was not given as much as a leaving card.

In fact, she could have retired with full pension rights a decade earlier. When reaching 60, the official retiring age, she was given a watch on the assumption that she would be leaving the Service. Retirement was not what Icolyn had in mind however, so she resumed working as a home help. As 65 approached and retirement was again discussed, she set herself a new target of 70, which she nearly achieved.

By then, however, the Soup Kitchen had been running for several years and she was still employed as a home help when she was awarded the MBE. Even though the honour had nothing to do with her job the Social Service was quick to write with congratulations for one of its own employees.

8

The Bishop

The area of East Oxford to the south of Cowley Road is characterised by narrow streets of small, terraced houses. In the middle of this dense housing and set in three acres of beautiful gardens is All Saints Convent. Occupied by the All Saints Sisters of the Poor, this unassuming order of nuns, dedicated to caring for the destitute and infirm, attracted national attention when its inspirational young mother superior founded Helen House, a hospice for children with terminal disease. The convent also shares its grounds with another of its institutions, St John's Home, which it describes as a residence for the elderly. In the early 1980s it became home to the retired Bishop George Appleton.

This eminent, intellectual and much-published cleric had served the Anglican Church among the poor of East London, in Burma, Perth, in Western Australia and in Jerusalem, where his mission was to protect and lead Anglican Arabs and Palestinians through one of the worst periods of the Israeli-Arab conflict. He was a man of deep spirituality with a longing for inter-faith tolerance and understanding. In retirement he became a pastoral councillor and, almost until his death, he received trainee priests for reflection and instruction. But such devotion had taken a toll on his family. He had become totally dependent on his wife for domestic management and, after her death, that responsibility fell to his unmarried daughter, Margaret.

For much of her adult life Margaret had been a secretary in Manchester but, in order to be near her father when he started living in the convent, she moved to Oxford and took up residence in a house he bought, 5 James Street. There she was able to fulfil her lifetime's ambition by embarking on a new career in interior design. At first she was employed by Stockland Dickens whose shop in Little

Clarendon Street had won a huge reputation locally for its extensive collection of furnishing fabrics and wall coverings. Under Jonathan Stockland's guidance her innate taste began to flourish and she was soon able to advise clients with confidence. It was experience which served her well because, when her father's increasing frailty compelled her to give up regular employment, she was able to go into business on her own account, offering design services from her home.

Starting any kind of business is stressful, and Margaret found that doing so while, at the same time, caring for her demanding father, even more so. George Appleton was still focused entirely on his devotions, almost to the exclusion of Margaret's welfare and his own health. Eventually her strength and self-confidence were sapped by the twin pressures of business and care and, unable any longer to cope on her own, she sought help from the Social Services.

Help came in the form of Icolyn Smith. At once she assessed the situation, saw how Margaret was worn down with worry, and that her father was likely to be a difficult client. She arrived every day at 6.30am to wash and dress him but it was becoming clear that the convent could no longer provide the kind of care that he needed. It was therefore decided that he should move into the James Street house with Margaret, where Icolyn continued with her morning duties for the next two years. 'I absolutely could not do without her,' says Margaret.

However, Icolyn was not impressed by what she found in James Street. Always alert to the household's needs, Margaret recalls with a laugh how, almost straight away, Icolyn told her to 'get new towels.' Later she advised her to give the Bishop a break from his daily dose of steroids because of the damage that prolonged use could cause. No problem there because he was a stubborn patient and Margaret often struggled to make him take his medication. However, with Icolyn around he 'took them like a lamb.' She was utterly dependable and had acquired the skill of being assertive without being offensive. Quietly and with confidence she helped Margaret deal with the practical difficulties of caring for her father.

*The James Street house where Margaret Appleton
lived with her father*

Although the Bishop had become used to people acquiescing to his demands he realised that Icolyn was someone who never took 'no' for an answer and that, in her, he had met his match. It became a relationship of mutual respect and when, later on, he heard about the Soup Kitchen, he told her about his own experiences in feeding the homeless in East London, and gave her £500 to help fund it.

Living now in her little cottage in Didcot, Margaret tells of how Icolyn confronted any problem with straightforward common sense, and dealt with it. As time passed the daily routine had to change as George Appleton became increasingly bed-bound. Avoiding bed

Bishop George Appleton

sores then became a concern but he was a well-built man and now rather bent, and Margaret found it difficult to turn him on her own. Seeing her struggle on one occasion, Icolyn immediately went out into the street 'to look for a strong man', returning almost immediately with a rather confused but undoubtedly strong student, on his way to the river for some early morning rowing practice. The job done, he was thanked and sent on his way within minutes. Margaret tells how, on another occasion, a group of rowdy teenagers was causing a disturbance in the street outside. Without hesitation, all five feet of Icolyn Smith marched outside, telling them that 'One day some of you will become doctors, and we will need to trust you'. They must have been so surprised that they didn't answer back; in any event, an equally surprised Margaret Appleton, watching from the window, saw them disperse quietly.

In the summer of 1993 the Bishop was tiring of the struggle for life and began to refuse his food. Margaret had difficulty in coping with the situation and turned to Icolyn for advice on what she should now do. Remembering one of her last conversations with Eric, Icolyn said 'Thank him for everything before it's too late.' This was not advice that Margaret was expecting. From her childhood in Burma to the expectations later on that she would be the one to care for her ailing parents, Margaret's life had been dominated by her father's wishes and his work. 'But,' she smiled 'I thought about it and found lots of things to thank him for.'

Arriving one day at her usual 6.30am, Icolyn was told that the Bishop had died in the night. Her calm resilience was shattered by the news and she burst into tears. A few days later, a distraught Margaret confided in her that she believed her father's refusal to take food amounted to a kind of suicide. 'Don't even think about it,' was Icolyn's advice.

9

One Morning in James Street

One day, not long after she had begun her morning visits to the Bishop, Icolyn had to make sure he was comfortable and smartly dressed because he was due to be visited by a group of trainee priests. This job done, she walked down James Street on her way to see her other clients. Just beyond the junction with St Mary's Road she noticed a young man scavenging for food in a concrete refuse bin. He had a violent tattoo along the length of his neck.

It was a turning point in her life. She was so shocked by what she saw that she prayed 'God – there must be something I can do to help people like him.' She remembers standing in the middle of the road,

It was just an ordinary concrete refuse bin

a road which at that time in the morning would normally be full of rush-hour traffic. But there was no traffic. And the sun, already shining brightly, suddenly glowed brighter still; then she became aware of a voice saying 'Feed them'. What clearer sign did she need?

When she got home that evening it was Gary who said 'Miss Brown – you've been talking about this for years – you'd better do something about it.' And she knew what to do. The following day she went to the Asian Cultural Centre in Manzil Way, formerly the chapel of the Cowley Road Hospital, and used at the time by the Church of God of Prophecy, her spiritual home. There she outlined her plans to the manager, Jawaid Malik. For reasons which she could never explain, she insisted that she wanted to use the Centre on Wednesdays – no other day would do. But that was when the Asian ladies used it for dress-making, so she was disappointed. However, that same evening Mr Malik telephoned her to say that the Asian ladies no longer needed it. 'God was there,' concluded Icolyn.

But she had no money. Neither did the Social Services where she worked. So she called in at the government offices in Tyndal House in Cowley Road. Though sympathetic to the need they, too, had no money. Then her telephone rang again. It was Tyndal House to say that £1500 had been found in an unspent budget. Suddenly things moved fast. Icolyn bought cooking pots from Taylor's in Littlemore, which are still in use today, and negotiated with Andy, the manager of Alder's, a family butcher in Cowley Road for the supply of fresh bones for boiling up stock. Mr Malik put notices in shops, pubs and hospitals. The Soup Kitchen was in business.

In the meantime the dedicated members of the Church of God of Prophecy rallied round in support. Icolyn had the drive and vision but none of the organisational experience necessary to run the kind of enterprise the Soup Kitchen was clearly becoming. It was agreed it would become one of the Church's community projects and many of the original helpers were drawn from the congregation. Among them was Sonia Brown, an accountant, who established some kind of financial order, and Pastor Grady Reid, who made the first application for a grant from the City Council. In those early days many organisations made donations including Oxfam, the European Union, Tesco, university colleges and student bodies. Despite a primary responsibility for ensuring the viability of the Asian Cultural Centre, achieved mainly through rental income, Jawaid Malik was assiduous in keeping costs down. All this enabled Icolyn to focus on serving Oxford's needy in the way she knew best. She was strict but fair and, as Pastor Reid recalls, 'what came out of her kitchen was always cooked with love.'

In the kitchen. Courtesy of Oxford Mail/The Oxford Times
(Newsquest Oxfordshire)

On the first day nine men came along, including the tattooed young man whose desperate scavenging inspired it all. It is symptomatic of the personal tragedy in those that Icolyn sought to help that he died two years later of a drug overdose. Anticipating more for the following Wednesday, she made a huge pot of soup and bought two sacks of potatoes. Word had got around and over 60 people came to be fed; they were dealt with in shifts and all were served. It was immediately clear that she was answering a desperate need, but Icolyn was still a full-time employee of the Social Services and the time she had taken in setting up the Soup Kitchen was deducted from her holiday allowance. This was clearly unsustainable so it was agreed that she could take Wednesdays off, unpaid.

Humanity in all its degradation and despair made the Wednesday Soup Kitchen its refuge. There were vagrants; people who had tried to make a go of it but had caved in under the pressures of modern living; others who were overwhelmed by marital and financial burdens; and then there were students, unprepared for a life away from home, who had sunk into drink and drugs. Most of them were men; all had lost hope and self-respect – and they stank. Occasionally there were women, sometimes so beyond caring that their menstruation was all too obvious. Icolyn addressed this new problem by collecting cast-off clothes. The Centre became busy as she encouraged people to use its hand-basins in the toilet, often their first wash in months, and to dispose of all their old clothes in a plastic bag for dumping. Sometimes it took only a clean body and clean clothes to make them feel better.

Icolyn knew the value of human contact. Unflinchingly she would embrace those who felt rejected and alone; grown men would cling to her and weep. They called her 'Ma' and hugged her. After a day at the Soup Kitchen she would go home sticky and smelly herself. And for this she said another little prayer: 'God, I thank you, because I have a home to go to, and can wash.'

Visiting the Soup Kitchen made people human again; it gave purpose to their lives and restored their self-respect. Simply knowing that someone actually cared about them made a difference. There are so many tales that Icolyn can tell about her 'people' but some, typical of many, are worth remembering; like the 19-yr old hoodie who sat silently in a corner until Icolyn put her arms around him. He rested his head on her chest and told her that he had no human contact for months; then he left without eating anything. Or the 17-yr old girl, an angry and drug-addled student whose boyfriend was in prison. Icolyn calmed her and through gentle encouragement,

The rules are strictly enforced.
Photograph: Harriet Browse

helped her get her life back on track; later her parents took her to Australia to make a new start.

But it soon became apparent that there must be rules: no swearing, no alcohol and no drugs; and dogs had to be left outside. Those who chose to ignore them had to stand up to the wrath of Icolyn and despite her diminutive size many a hard man has backed down. Many more have been transformed, regained their self-confidence and found a purpose in life. And some such as Charlie, the subject of a separate chapter, became helpers themselves.

10

East Meets West

The distance between Kingston and Oxford is about 4500 miles. Almost as far, but in the opposite direction, is the ancient city of Sialkot, in the far north-east of Pakistan and close to the disputed territory of Kashmir. Its recorded history stretches back centuries before it was invaded by Alexander the Great and became the eastern-most outpost of the Hellenic Empire. Today, Sialkot is a large, industrial city with an international reputation for the manufacture of surgical instruments, sports equipment and leather garments – 70 per cent of the world's hand-sewn footballs are made there. After Karachi, Sialkot is Pakistan's largest source of foreign exchange.

However, its prosperity and security have been under threat since independence from Britain in 1947 which divided the sub-continent into mainly-Muslim Pakistan and mainly-Hindu India. Just as Icolyn was making her journey from Kingston to Oxford, the two countries were at war, and the biggest tank battle since El Alamein took place a few miles from Sialkot. The city was successfully defended by the Pakistani army but not before it had been bombarded, with many casualties, and much of the civilian population had been forced to flee.

Among them was Jawaid Malik, just twelve years old at the time, whose extended family was involved in a variety of businesses across the city. When the seventeen-day war ended in stalemate he was able to return to school and then go on to obtain a diploma in mechanical engineering. Although he might well have been expected to work in one of the family businesses he decided to join a group of progressive activists who devoted themselves to the social development of their young nation. He helped establish a model village and a network of sports facilities throughout the country. But, at the age of 30, he felt the need for new challenges and joined his brother in Leicester. He had moved there some years earlier and had become involved in promoting inter-faith understanding between Muslim, Hindu and Sikh immigrants and the wider Christian English community.

As in the Caribbean, immigration from Pakistan to Britain was precipitated in the 1960s by the lure of relatively well-paid jobs; many came from the Kashmir region where over 100,000 people had been displaced by the construction of a huge dam and reservoir. However, as Icolyn experienced herself, they were often unwelcome and suffered verbal and more serious abuse at the hands of skinheads, the National Front and other right-wing elements. Immigration from the sub-continent was mainly by young men who would occupy a lodging house, taking turns with the limited sleeping space and with the cooking, washing and cleaning for the whole household. Although such houses became very crowded, there was safety in numbers and the costs were low, enabling those who worked hard to send money back home and accumulate some capital for themselves.

By the time Jawaid arrived in Leicester harmony between immigrants of Indian and Pakistani origin had been restored but there was still much to be done in building a community that integrated with the native British population. His brother had become a trade union leader and active in local politics, and welcomed Jawaid's help in dealing with the constant flow of problems presented by those individuals having difficulty in adjusting to unfamiliar cultures. It was experience that served him well because five years later he applied for, and was appointed, manager of the new Asian Cultural Centre in Oxford, and there he met Icolyn Smith.

The Asian Cultural Centre is housed in a disused chapel, all that is left of the Cowley Road Hospital that was demolished in 1986 and where Icolyn worked some 20 years earlier. Located behind a small park just across the road from her Randolph Street house it was available for hire by the wider community, and Icolyn's church, the Church of God of Prophecy was one of its tenants at the time. The park retained some of the old apple trees and potting sheds from the hospital's kitchen garden and was occupied at night by many of Oxford's derelicts and outcasts. Used needles and human excreta made it an unhealthy place, particularly for children for whom it was the only open place in which to play. But it was this shifting population of lost souls that Icolyn felt compelled to help.

It was a need that Jawaid recognised as soon as he took up his new post. He had been shocked to discover that, unlike Leicester, Oxford's elitism had created a fragmented community whose casual indifference did little to alleviate the squalor of its homeless. Asian cultures have similar problems of domestic, financial and mental crisis but it is the tradition for friends and family to rally round, so such public degradation is rarely seen. He was therefore anxious to help Icolyn, was inspired by her passion, and soon found himself working long hours for a community that was not Asian.

Oxford City Council owns the Asian Cultural Centre and employed Jawaid to manage it under the guidance of the Oxford Asian Cultural Association. Then, as now, it ran keep-fit, sewing and Asian-language classes and a weekly lunch club, but they contributed little in rent. And neither could a Soup Kitchen which had precious few resources itself and which attracted an unwashed clientele for whom a good meal was just one of their many needs. Persuading the Association to accept yet another heavily-discounted tenant was the first of many challenges that Jawaid recalls. However, convinced that these difficulties could be overcome, he went about alerting Oxford's homeless to this new facility despite the uncertainty about how many would respond and how they might behave.

By the second Wednesday the need was clear when at least 60 came to the Soup Kitchen. No-one was turned away and, somehow, Icolyn managed to produce a meal for everyone. This presented Jawaid with further problems. Such success required catering and storage facilities that the Centre did not have but, with typical ingenuity, he overcame them. It then became evident that a wider service was needed: many people arrived wearing the only clothes they possessed, so the Soup Kitchen also became a distribution centre for second-hand clothes; there were also handouts of soap and toiletries, including razors for men and tampons for women. Soon, however, it became noticeable that people who had lost all self-respect were beginning to take care of themselves, their hygiene and appearance. It was the beginning of a long road which, over the years, has been tramped by thousands. It has helped many people on it to rebuild their lives and some of them have gone on to find work, careers, get married and have families.

A generation in age and origins from different continents separate Icolyn and Jawaid but they are one of a kind. Both have a feisty determination to get things done and both have a deep concern for the welfare of people who are in such desperate need. Jawaid remembers having long, philosophical discussions with Icolyn on the meaning of humanity and spirituality. He acquired a respect and affection for her which he likens to that between a man and his mother; from her he learned the importance of human contact and how something as simple as a hug somehow makes difficulties evaporate. To be hugged by Icolyn is one of life's privileges.

11

A Meeting with Royalty

It was not the kind of letter you receive every day. At the top was a crest with a coat of arms including the lion and unicorn, and below that was the address: 10 Downing Street, London. Then there was the date: 13 November 1998. Icolyn couldn't make it out so she passed the letter to Blossom, who studied it more carefully. 'Dear Madam' it began 'The Prime Minister has asked me to inform you, in strict confidence, that he has it in mind, on the occasion of the forthcoming list of New Year Honours, to submit your name to The Queen with a recommendation that Her Majesty may be graciously pleased to approve that you be appointed a Member of the Order of the British Empire.'

This was stunning news. How could the Prime Minister know about Icolyn? She had already been awarded a Certificate of Honour from the Lord Mayor of Oxford and that was totally unexpected. But this . . .! The letter continued: 'Before doing so, the Prime Minister would be glad to be assured that this would be acceptable to you.' Of course it was acceptable and she lost no time in returning the form that came with the letter.

It is almost impossible to keep such a momentous event bottled up, but that is what the family managed to do until the New Year's Honours List of 1998 was published. The response was immediate. The Oxford Mail was among the first to call and the article it published resulted in a torrent of telephone calls, letters and cards of congratulation. Most were from people who Icolyn knew but some were from acquaintances she had not seen for years. One was from Mrs Vera Woodley who worked with her at Cowley Road Hospital a quarter of a century earlier. There were letters from the Lord Mayor of Oxford and from the Director of Social Services at

The original letter from 10 Downing Street

Oxfordshire County Council, where Icolyn was still employed as a home help.

Kelburne Road was rarely in the news but, suddenly, all its residents felt able to enjoy the honour of their famous neighbour. It was a common talking point which perceptively raised community spirit and engendered a feeling of pride. There was pride and happiness in the Soup Kitchen too. Everyone – both helpers and 'my people' as Icolyn called those in the dining room – shared in the reflected glory.

All at once, everyone seemed to know her. Her photograph in the Oxford Mail, enlarged to poster size in its office window in New Inn Hall Street, and displayed as well in Cowley Centre, meant that she was instantly recognizable. Wherever she went she was surrounded by well-wishers; she was greeted by complete strangers and she could see people whispering and pointing her out to each other. This unfamiliar celebrity was intrusive but it was a price she paid willingly because, in her words 'This is for everybody'. In any case it lasted only a few weeks before the resumption of life's routine.

The investiture was to be held on 20 May 1999 but as the weeks of winter edged slowly towards spring with no further communication from either Downing Street or the Palace, Blossom felt compelled to find out more information. It had been a long time since that first letter arrived. Supposing something had been lost in the post? Maybe Icolyn had somehow dropped off the list? She need not have worried though. It seems this is a common experience and most people telephone to ask about the arrangements, and what they are expected to do. Then more specific instructions arrived from the Central Chancery of the Orders of Knighthood, including the important matter of what to wear.

In some things Icolyn is not easily satisfied and Blossom took her on several expeditions to Oxford's department stores before she found what she wanted. Eventually, a particularly helpful assistant in Debenhams steered her towards the perfect choice: a silver-grey two-piece with a stone-coloured hat and matching handbag. For her own outfit, Blossom took a day off work to scour Oxford Street, in London.

When the big day arrived they travelled in two cars – Icolyn, Blossom and Lorna with Norman driving in the first, with George and June close behind. To make sure they arrived in good time they had made arrangements to spend the night in a small hotel near the Palace, and when the manager learned about the purpose of their visit he was nearly as excited as they were.

The invitation to the Investiture was for 'Mrs Icolyn Smith and three guests' so, the next morning, Norman, George and Blossom went to the Palace in Norman's car while Lorna and June remained in the hotel. They had been told that the Palace gates would be opened at 10.00 am precisely and when they got there, they found that a parking space had already been allocated for them in front of the Palace itself. Icolyn was directed to the Picture Gallery where those to be awarded honours were given an official welcome and were told about the procedure by the Lord Chamberlain. There she learned that the Queen was attending to other duties at Windsor Castle so the Prince of Wales would be deputising for her. In the meantime the guests were offered refreshments in the Green Hall, a large, ornately decorated space guarded by a uniformed usher standing stiffly to attention. Blossom thought he was a statue until he moved. While they were there, she went to inspect the Ladies, hoping to find something rather special, but she was disappointed. For the record, they are old fashioned with large, wooden seats; and instead of being embossed with the Royal coat-of-arms as one might expect, the toilet paper is of standard supermarket quality.

The ceremony itself was enacted with military precision, unsurprising since it was run by military men. Everyone was seated in the Ballroom while the orchestra of the Grenadier Guards played selections from popular classics. At precisely 11.00 am they played the National Anthem, a signal for everyone to rise as Prince Charles entered with an escort of Ghurka officers. He made his way to a dais behind which five members of The Queen's Body Guard of the Yeomen of the Guard stood stiffly to attention. The Lord Chamberlain then announced each recipient in turn; they were expected to bow or curtsey to the Prince, according to their gender, step forward for him to present them with their insignia and to exchange a few words. He then shook their hand, a signal that their time was up and they would step back a few paces, before bowing or curtseying again.

When it came to be Icolyn's turn His Royal Highness said 'We cannot pay for the work you have done, but this is a token of our appreciation.' This was probably the standard script but he then asked her, with a twinkle in his eye 'Do you give them some of that hot stuff?' Prince Charles had experienced the spicy dishes of the Caribbean and Icolyn confirmed that they were sometimes on the menu at the Soup Kitchen. This charming moment is captured on video showing a smiling Prince bending over Icolyn in genuine affection and admiration.

Despite the formality, it was a surprisingly relaxed occasion. After the ceremony, all 132 people who had been honoured that day rejoined their guests to share the experience in animated conversation. There were people there from all walks of life and every part of the UK, but they all had one thing in common – they had done something exceptional, and had the privilege of being citizens of a country that recognised achievement in this unique way.

By 12.15 pm it was all over. The only problem was that Icolyn could not be found. She was eventually discovered deep in conversation with a Palace official. Then a policeman told Blossom that unless she stopped taking photographs she would be locked in, because he had to close the gates. While all this had been going on, George's car had been subject to the attentions of a parking warden but even the ticket fixed firmly to the windscreen failed to mar the excitement of the occasion. It was mid-afternoon by the time they

*Icolyn outside Buckingham Palace with her newly-
awarded MBE*

got back to Oxford; there were photographs of the family taken against the backdrop of the beautiful garden belonging to Mr & Mrs Harris, Icolyn's neighbours in Kelburne Road, and everyone stayed for a pizza supper and to talk, long into the evening, about the day's momentous events.

And then, of course, there was another celebration, in the Asian Cultural Centre. As well as her extended family, guests included friends who had known Icolyn over the years, helpers and her 'people' in the Soup Kitchen. It was Icolyn and Blossom who did most of the catering, maintaining their strict no-alcohol policy, except for the Jamaican fruit cake, in which a good measure of rum is an essential ingredient. Icolyn showed her guests the MBE, proudly displayed in its presentation box. But that didn't seem quite right, so someone took it out of the box and put it where it should be – pinned to her dress.

Winston Churchill stated that the honours were 'to give pride and pleasure to those who deserve them'. Icolyn's MBE gave pride and pleasure to a great many people. It was later revealed that she had been nominated for the award by Tim Kelly, who was caretaker at the Asian Cultural Centre, with help from Frank Isaacs, its secretary.

The MBE is now proudly framed on the wall of her sitting room along with a Certificate of Honour from the Lord Mayor of Oxford, awarded in 2000, the Deborah Award of 2008 from the Church of God of Prophecy and an Oxfordshire Charity & Volunteer Award, presented in 2013.

12

The First Big Thing in Cowley Road

In the late 1990s the area around Cowley Road was classified among the most deprived urban areas in the country. This stimulated a community group calling itself East Oxford Action to campaign for rejuvenation of the area giving rise to a number of projects. Among them was the Carnival which Icolyn describes as 'The first big thing to happen in Cowley Road'. For one day in July Cowley Road now bursts with noise, colour, people, music and dancing and it attracts so many people that the road has to be closed. Although its origins go back 30 years it was not until 2001 that it came to life in its present form, apart from two years in which financial and logistical difficulties forced a move to South Park. The Carnival has grown every year and nearly 30,000 people now come as spectators or participants in a day of joyous, uninhibited celebration.

To begin with the Carnival was based on that patch of open space next to Manzil Way and opposite Randolph Street, which features elsewhere in this book. Murals were painted on some of the nearby buildings which are still visible today. There was music from rock bands, African percussion and samba; there were Indian dance groups and a Chinese dragon, all reflecting the diversity and culture of those from many lands who had made the Cowley Road area their home. Such was its success that in the following year there was a procession along the road's length involving over 300 people – musicians and dancers, including school children; there was even a Carnival Queen. Today it attracts people from all over Oxford and beyond.

In 2013 it was even bigger and better. Gary, performing under his professional name of DJG, was one of several disc jockeys stationed

The Cowley Road Carnival. Photograph: David Turner

along the route of the procession. The day was warm, the colours bright, the costumes magnificent and the noise terrific. No less than 32 groups, involving over 600 people, were involved in the procession as it played, sang and danced its way up the road. At its head were some honoured local heroes – and among them was Icolyn Smith.

Much of the planning for the Carnival requires the provision of services, including catering, for the large influx of people. To meet the need, Icolyn has always had a stall for takeaway food – curry, chicken and rice, provided at cost by the neighbouring shops and restaurants. And for days leading up to the event, Icolyn and Blossom are busy baking. The stall is, in itself, no small undertaking, requiring a start as early at 6.00 am to get everything ready, and most of the family get involved. Although much of the food is prepared in advance, it is actually cooked in the kitchen of the Asian Cultural Centre, which is nearby, or in the stall itself, requiring gas and cookers to be brought it. It is served from tables under a colourful gazebo, and is always busy.

Although the Carnival is a community event it has to be run on business lines. In 2013 it cost around nearly £100,000 of which £24,000 alone was spent on road closures and security. These costs are met by grants from the City Council, sponsorship by some of Oxford's principal employers and donations from local businesses. Even that is insufficient to cover everything so further income is derived from renting space to stall-holders like Icolyn. She also has to pay for insurance and the hire of equipment. Even so she can clear up to £3000, money which she divides between the Soup Kitchen and another cause dear to the heart, the Children's Hospital at the John Radcliffe Hospital.

Icolyn in her stall at the 2014 Cowley Road
Carnival, waiting for the procession to arrive.
She had been up since 6.00am to get things ready

Icolyn had always been concerned that although Oxford was well-provided with excellent hospitals and a leading medical school, seriously ill children had to go elsewhere for specialist treatment, often to Great Ormond Street Hospital in London. She was therefore delighted to learn of the proposals to include a dedicated children's hospital in the expansion of the John Radcliffe Hospital following the closure of the old Radcliffe Infirmary in central Oxford.

The hospital itself opened in 2007 although the process of designing and building it began many years earlier, with many appeals to help finance it. Icolyn's response was to organise a distribution of collection tins – marked Little People with Big Needs – in many of the Cowley Road shops, whose contents she took regularly to the John Radcliffe's fundraising office. Every Saturday morning, for several years, she stood outside Tesco in Cowley Road with a collection bucket; later she was to collect outside Sainsbury's in Helford Hill as well. Used effectively, those buckets can collect a lot of money in a short time. Icolyn was well known, of course, and people donated their change readily, but she was not above using the strength of her personality to shame others into doing so. She remembers telling a smartly-dressed young man who was trying to avoid eye-contact 'I am too old to have more children but you aren't, and they may need our new hospital.' His donation was not loose change, but notes.

Simple arithmetic suggests that, over the years, Icolyn has been personally responsible for raising tens of thousands for the Children's Hospital.

13

Will You be My Mum?

Moments before he had been standing in solitary disdain, watching the others queuing in the Soup Kitchen. If life had treated him more kindly he would have been a good-looking man. Despite his ill-fitting clothes, beard and long hair he had evidently put some effort into his appearance; his upright bearing suggested an aloofness and his alert watchfulness, a wary distrust. Charlie had been there before. The first time he came, just a few weeks earlier, he had watched for a while, then walked away without taking anything. Icolyn had seen his sort before; it was usually pride that prevented them from accepting the charity on offer. When he next appeared, still standing apart, Icolyn went up to him and touched his sleeve; he flinched away, staring at her angrily. But, grudgingly, he accepted the box of food she offered, and left.

This time, Icolyn put her arms around him and, astonished and overwhelmed, he burst into tears. That simple act had found a soul he did not know he possessed. Hard, proud Charlie who, in all his 40 years, had never experienced human kindness, was suddenly humiliated. Years of pent-up anger and resentment flowed out in convulsive sobs. To an outsider it would have been disconcerting to see them clinging to each other like that but, in that haven of hope, where so many had known desperation, it was not unusual to see Icolyn rescue people in this way. They had many needs and Icolyn was always ready to do what she could to help, but Charlie's request was different. Still struggling to control his emotions, the first words he said to Icolyn were 'Will you be my Mum?'

At the age of 14 Charlie was living rough in London's East End and had started drinking; some time earlier he had run away from home and school, and no-one seemed to care. It was almost inevitable that he would drift towards the underworld of petty criminals, drunks and losers; soon he became caught up in the dangerous web of the Kray Brothers, twins who terrorised London in the fifties and sixties. Their speciality was armed robbery, extortion and intimidation, backed up by unrestrained violence. To be a member of The Firm, as the Krays' associates were called, was an honour which had to be earned by unhesitating obedience. Membership brought self-respect, of a sort, but reduced human relationships to simple fear. It made Charlie hard, arrogant and unapproachable.

Charlie became a pawn in The Firm and was put to work in the newly-emerging markets for illegal drugs. He became a dealer, and soon he was hooked himself. The Krays' reign finally came to an end in 1968 with their arrest on three counts of murder and many in the Firm went down too as their empire unravelled. It was every man for himself, as former colleagues in crime sought to compromise each other, as the net closed in. Many escaped and now live ordinary

The demise of the Kray twins, as reported in the Daily Mail on 9 May 1968

lives, harbouring some devastating secrets for more than half a century.

Charlie was one of the lucky ones, probably because of his youth. Like everyone else, he disappeared for a while, but soon he was back on the streets, re-establishing links with his former clients and building new ones; he was in business. The hedonism of the Swinging Sixties had made cannabis in all its forms almost commonplace in London's pubs and clubs. Many of its users were demanding a stronger high and experimented with heroin and cocaine. They became hooked and found themselves on the slope to destruction and degradation, and Charlie was there to help them on their way.

To Charlie, the sale of drugs to willing clients was an occupation that put him well above the riff-raff who chose theft and violence as a way of living. Later, he was to boast that he had never stolen anything from anyone – and had never been arrested. He was too clever for that. But not clever enough to rise though the shadowy hierarchy of the supply chain, where the real money was made. He had tried, of course, and had the scars to prove it; on one occasion he was so badly injured that a frightened passer-by called an ambulance, but Charlie managed to get away before it arrived. Hospitals meant questions and the kind of questions he would be asked meant the police. So he settled for the quiet life, dealing discreetly with a group of long-term, hopeless addicts, cultivating their dependency on him.

He had no pity for whose lives he was destroying; after all, he could so easily have been one of them. He was unmoved by their squalor, unconcerned about how they got the cash to pay him. They needed him, desperately, and the power this gave him caused his self-esteem to rise accordingly.

No-one asks questions in the Soup Kitchen so how it was that Charlie came to Oxford – why, or even when – remains a mystery. Clearly he had made an effort to live a normal life because he had got married and fathered a son. But the marriage did not last and his wife went back to her home in Scotland, taking their son with her. Probably he resumed the only business he knew, this time in Oxford.

| 77 |

He became a gruff, intimidating outcast; most of the shops in Cowley Road refused to serve him. But things were not going well; he was poisoning himself as well as others and his own life was sliding into chaos. It was only a matter of time before he turned up at the Soup Kitchen.

During their long embrace Icolyn whispered that there was work that needed doing in the kitchen. Would Charlie like to help her? Charlie had never helped anyone in his life. This was something completely new – no need for cunning or deceit, no place for menace. It was simple work, work which the helpers in the kitchen would have done anyway but, after some hesitation, Charlie joined them. In the kitchen he met people whose goodwill was overflowing, some of them with tragedies of their own; people who were not motivated by crude self-interest. The experience was a long-delayed turning point in his life.

During the weeks that followed he came regularly but not to take his place in the shabby, shuffling queue of those in need but to join the team of helpers. He took charge of the dining room upstairs, putting up the tables and chairs, laying out the cutlery and storing everything away afterwards. He was always alert to signs of trouble, and trouble sometimes happened. Usually it was something that Icolyn was more than capable of handling herself, but now Charlie stepped in: 'She's my Mum – don't you speak to her like that.' Unlikely though this may have seemed, he confronted men much bigger than himself with as much vehemence as if it was true. His devotion became like a dog that never leaves its master's side. For the next 15 years he was one of the Soup Kitchen's most reliable helpers and, without having to be asked, he would do any job that needed doing. He never forgot Icolyn at Christmas – or on Mother's Day. He gave her flowers, not on the Sunday itself, but at the Wednesday Soup Kitchen because he wanted his present to be her first.

He once told Icolyn 'Only one person could get the Charlie out of me – and that person was you.' A new self-respect made him reappraise his life and he disciplined himself to give up smoking, drinking and drugs. He even enrolled at Ruskin College. Ruskin is

*Charlie Buscott. Courtesy of
Oxford Mail/The Oxford Times
(Newsquest Oxfordshire)*

an independent college that specialises in providing educational
opportunities for adults with few or no qualifications. It aims to
offer a second chance at education; for Charlie it was his first chance.
After a year he gained a Certificate in Higher Education, the first
praiseworthy achievement he had ever known. Bursting with a form
of pride he had never before experienced, he insisted that Icolyn
should join him in the awards ceremony.

It was a new, reformed Charlie who used his qualification to find
work with the probation service. He became a well-known figure
among Oxford's homeless, working not just at the Soup Kitchen but
at The Gap in Park End Street and the Gatehouse in St Giles' Church.
He had direct experience of the demons and despair brought on by
drink and drugs; he knew life at its hardest and lowest. It became his
mission to rescue people as Icolyn had rescued him. She even taught
him how to pray.

Helpers in the Soup Kitchen come from all walks of life and Charlie's story is far from unique. At the other extreme there are professional people like Nick who, for many years, combined his voluntary service with his work as an optician. It was Nick who came to Charlie's aid when, once again, he had to face the prospect of homelessness. Charlie had been living in Divinity Road but some kind of crisis occurred in which he was told to leave. This sudden insecurity could easily have tipped him back into his old ways. He did not have the kind of record which landlords wanted but, with guarantees from Nick, a flat was found for him in Botley Road.

Charlie's life returned to the routine of work among Oxford's disadvantaged but always and without fail, Wednesdays in the Soup Kitchen. Then, in 2010, he woke up one morning and found that he had no control over his left arm; it just hung limply by his side. Icolyn made him go to the doctor who immediately referred him to the John Radcliffe Hospital for an X-ray. It was an anxious time waiting for the results. Charlie, who was always careful with his appearance, now found that he could not even dress himself. In great distress, he rang Icolyn to say that he might not be able to come to the Soup Kitchen for much longer, and for the second time while talking to her, this tough, bold man began to cry. Icolyn felt so helpless; there seemed nothing she could do.

The diagnosis was cancer; in the lungs and in the brain where the tumour was affecting the nerve to his left arm. When Icolyn telephoned him the following Wednesday he told her that he was alright but, on the next day, an ambulance was called to take him to the hospital again. She and Gary went up to see him but he was so heavily sedated that he was unaware of their presence. Then Gary had a telephone call from a stranger who revealed himself to be Charlie's son who he had not seen for 16 years. He had been to see Charlie and found him conscious and cheerful. That reunion came just in time because within 24 hours, Charlie's life had slipped away.

It was only with the loss of Charlie that Icolyn realised how close they had become. Decades earlier she had raised her own family of five, into which, at the age of nine, Hilroy had drifted and stayed;

then, much later, she had become Charlie's adopted mother. And Charlie had been the first to go. Her distress was compounded by a call from Charlie's nephew. Could she give the address at the funeral? It was what Charlie would have wanted. In all this time he had never spoken of his family but only then did it emerge that he was still in touch with them and had told them all about Icolyn.

Oxford Crematorium is a bleak, cheerless place; because of its function it could hardly be otherwise. Quite a few of 'the boys' from the Soup Kitchen attended the funeral, along with Icolyn, Blossom and Gary, and helpers Gloria and Margaret. Then there was Charlie's family, who clustered around Icolyn as if they had always known her. Gary had to support her as she struggled to say a few words about Charlie's life and as the curtain closed across the coffin, she could hardly stifle a scream of grief. Charlie had chosen the music himself: 'Don't search for me – I'm in the arms of the angels.'

14

A Surprise Visitor

No-one knows, not even Icolyn, who will be coming to the Soup Kitchen until they actually arrive. There is the solid, but small core of helpers who can always be relied on, but often more arrive without warning so that the kitchen sometimes becomes congested with too many people. They could be students or, sometimes, American servicemen from RAF Croughton, who have provided help several times over the years. Others call in simply to donate food, clothes or money. The staff at the Registry Office are typical of

Tim Stevenson, Lord Lieutenant of Oxfordshire, in floral apron with Icolyn and Gary. Courtesy of Oxford Mail/The Oxford Times (Newsquest Oxfordshire)

those who make collections throughout the year and deliver the proceeds from time to time.

Occasionally there have been 'official visits' by dignitaries who come to show their support. But Icolyn sees to it that everyone plays their part; there is no room in the kitchen for people to be simply on-lookers while all the voluntary helpers are working so hard. Thus it was that no exception was made on the occasion of a visit by Tim Stevenson. As Lord Lieutenant of Oxfordshire, he may be the official representative of the Queen, but that did not stop Icolyn fitting him out with a floral apron within minutes of his arrival. For the next two hours he was washing the cooking pans by hand and serving in the dining room.

In the dining room itself there is a similar situation; there is always a large group of regulars, some of whom have been coming for years, supplemented by another, unpredictable number of Icolyn's 'people'. For some it may be their first visit, having heard about the good food and companionship through the grape-vine. They may come once or for a few weeks, sometimes to disappear again, perhaps to return sometime later.

It is not unusual for another category of visitors to arrive, usually by arrangement. Sometimes there are people on work experience; they could be from local charities or from the Council. The press knows about the Soup Kitchen well and its reporters and photographers come unobtrusively when preparing an article for the Oxford Mail or its sister publications. Gary has worked for Radio Oxford so the BBC knows about it too. Sometimes students come along; in the early days they came as helpers but now they might be training as healthcare or social workers, or perhaps they are on courses in media studies for which the Soup Kitchen might be a suitable project. Of course, all such visitors have to be very discrete and respect the privacy of everyone there.

It was therefore not out of the ordinary when, in November 2011, a request came in for the Soup Kitchen to be included in a television documentary to be called 'Food for Thought', showing how sharing food can bring people together. On the agreed day two people came to talk to Icolyn and her team, and to some of the people in the dining room. Two weeks later they returned with a film crew. As they were leaving they mentioned that they would like to introduce Icolyn to a friend who worked as a taxi driver but who was considering a new career in catering and was interested in helping in the kitchen. Then there was a busy few days: on the Monday they wanted to feature the process of receiving and sorting the donated clothes; on the Tuesday, while Icolyn was preparing the vegetables for the following day they all came to lunch at Kelburne Road; and on the Wednesday everyone was in the Soup Kitchen, with the taxi driver washing the dishes. He was introduced to Icolyn as Nats and as far as she was concerned he had a lot to learn and she told him so, but he was, after all, only a beginner.

On the Friday Nats called in to see Icolyn at Kelburne Road. While he was standing at the door he held her hand tightly. 'Why are you doing that? she asked. 'Because I've been lying to you and I'm afraid you might hit me.' He then told her that his real name was Arfan Razak, a self-made entrepreneur who had been commissioned by Chanel 4 to go undercover in Oxford for an episode in its reality TV series the *Secret Millionaire*. Raz, as he was commonly known, had brought with him the necessary release forms and if she agreed to sign them he would make a substantial donation to the Soup Kitchen's funds.

On a personal level, Raz said that he had been deeply moved by his experience at the Soup Kitchen; for the first time in his life he had come face-to-face with poverty, and with someone who devoted herself so unflinchingly to helping the needy. Raz had always worked hard and played hard; he lived life in the fast lane and measured success only by material possessions. In working on this project he had met people whose standards were totally different, and he felt ashamed by his previous indifference to those whose luck had run out. While he had been making the programme in Oxford, his producers had found Raz a squalid little room to live in, so small he could almost touch each wall when he stood in the middle, but for some of those who came to the Soup Kitchen it would have seemed like luxury.

Icolyn was stunned by the news. The *Secret Millionaire* was one of her favourite programmes but she never dreamed that she might appear in it herself. She was annoyed by the deception but quickly realised how the additional publicity could benefit the Soup Kitchen. And what was that about 'a sizable donation'? She was soon to find out.

Gary's reaction was the same. 'I don't know whether to hug you or punch you' he told Raz. For the next three months it was Gary who became his local contact point and who met him on the two or three occasions when the production team had to return to Oxford to complete the programme. Transmission was scheduled for 7 May 2012 and until then the entire project and particularly the 'sizable donation' had to be kept secret. It was not easy to stay silent when something so exciting was happening but Icolyn and the family had managed to do it before – during the interval between the private and public announcements about her award of the MBE.

In the meantime they learned more about their remarkable benefactor. Raz was born in Pakistan and was brought to the UK by his parents when he was less than a year old. His father worked all hours of the day and into the night as a taxi driver in order to provide a future for his family in their new homeland. He believed that education was the key to success and was determined that Raz would go to university and embark on a career in the professions. Raz chose medicine but the long training was interrupted by a car accident which disabled and demoralised him, and delayed his studies by several months. When he gained his degree he decided that his future lay in industry and over the next few years he worked for several pharmaceutical companies, eventually rising to sales director. He was soon earning good money but he still felt unfulfilled and looked for a new challenge. Almost on impulse he bought a city-centre restaurant in his home town of Nottingham, hoping to turn it into something rather special. That was in 2005; he had no business experience and had never been in catering. That showed when the Curry Lounge first opened in 2007 and was given a drubbing by Gordon Ramsay on another Channel 4 reality programme, *Kitchen*

Nightmares. However, Raz learned from the experience and he quickly gave the restaurant a new focus which emphasised quality at a reasonable price. It is now listed among the UK's top curry restaurants and is rated the best city-centre restaurant in Nottingham.

But still success did not satisfy his restless energies and he began supporting charities, particularly in mental health. Raz knew how debilitating the condition could be; he had suffered from depression himself following the car crash, and his mother suffered from it too. At the same time he was also supporting a charity for the Royal Marines. In that he sought sponsorship to undertake an exercise known as the dunker, which required him to escape from deep water while strapped into a simulated helicopter that had crashed and overturned. All this came to the attention of the producers of the *Secret Millionaire*. They needed an enterprising, generous individual to work on a project among the disadvantaged of Oxford and Raz seemed to fit the bill. But there was a condition for doing so: he was expected to make a substantial, personal donation to the organisations he worked with.

When the final edits had been made for the *Secret Millionaire* Raz invited Icolyn and her family to a screening in the Curry Lounge, one hour in advance of its transmission. The production team and other media were there in strength but it was a big party for Raz himself because he had become a well-known personality in Nottingham. However Icolyn felt she was being treated like royalty as Raz introduced her to everyone else. At one point his wife asked her 'What did you do to my husband? He's a changed person!' The screening was held in a casino above the restaurant and afterwards there was a fabulous spread of Asian and British food. It was a very glamorous occasion which overwhelmed and exhausted Icolyn; they did not get back to Oxford until 3.00am the next morning.

In the Channel 4 transmission Raz plays the enthusiastic amateur to perfection; indeed the Oxford Mail reported that the *Secret Millionaire* was seen 'being given a dressing down by the famously no-nonsense Mrs Smith.' There was no nonsense, either, about Raz's donation of £11,500 to the Soup Kitchen's funds. Most people

Icolyn and Raz at the screening of the Secret Millionaire

would have used the opportunity to invest in efficiencies which might make its operation less demanding on the team that ran it, but that wasn't Icolyn's way. She knew that her 'people' had few places to go to on Saturdays so, at the age of 82, she opened the Soup Kitchen for a second day every week.

It was almost like receiving the MBE all over again as Icolyn became a local celebrity for a few weeks. The telephone started ringing at 8.00am on the morning after the broadcast; there were letters and cards of congratulation, and complete strangers stopped to talk to her in the street. But it was in the Soup Kitchen, among some emotional scenes, that appreciation was most strongly felt. She had drawn attention to all those people who had so little self-esteem and little of anything else, and they were grateful.

15

Prayer is Part of My Life

Icolyn begins the day, quietly on her own in the front room at Kelburne Road, with an hour of prayer, Bible-reading and reflection. She thanks God for bringing her another day and offers prayers for her family and for others she knows to be in need of help. Many of the most desperate at the Soup Kitchen have asked her to pray for them and although she has never attempted to lead them towards the Church, there are some who have followed her example and become Christians. Many times in her life prayer has been the answer to her own despair. After Eric's death she felt very much alone and overwhelmed with the responsibility of managing the mortgage and providing for her family, particularly for her young son Gary. Then she distinctly remembers feeling an arm around her shoulder and an audible voice saying 'I will never leave you.' Convinced it was reassurance from God, Icolyn has become a firm believer in the power of prayer.

As with so many people from the Caribbean, the Christian faith was always part of Icolyn's life. On Sundays, Coolshade was almost deserted because nearly everyone had gone to the church in Gubay. Those who were not regular church-goers were mainly men, her father George Brown among them, but the entire community always came together to celebrate the Christian festivals. Even the poorest, perhaps scratching a living deep in the countryside, would arrive; men in an immaculate dark suit, white shirt and polished shoes and the women in their brightest and best. However it was the school which established a life-long adherence to Christian values; there was a prayer at the beginning and end of every day – 'If I have wounded any soul today, good Lord forgive me'; and the grace after lunch was 'Thank you Lord for everything.' Religious education was

Icolyn's Bible

a fundamental part of the curriculum, reinforced by the church to which the school was physically attached, and by its Sunday School services.

Both the church and Sunday School at Gubay were run by the Church of England whose ministers, trained in the sterile rituals of the mother country, found a congregation that was devoted and exuberant. It comes as a shock, therefore, to learn that in the 1960s the Church of England was not welcoming to those who had emigrated to this country, and politely but firmly told those who attended their services to find a church more appropriate to their background.

When Icolyn moved to Kingston the bright lights and excitement of urban life loosened the ties of her faith. Although still committed, she did not join any particular congregation and her attendance at church services became infrequent. But the onset of parenthood drew the bonds tighter with the realisation that the Church offered a beacon of security among the problems and uncertainties of Kingston. Icolyn needed that feeling of security, too, when she took the long journey to rejoin Eric in Oxford. Her relationship with the Almighty was a personal one and still did not express itself in a regular Sunday service, but she found comfort and reassurance in occasional visits to the John Bunyan Baptist Church, the Pentecostal Church in St Clements and others in the area of Cowley Road. So when a stranger knocked on the door of their Randolph Street home to ask for directions to the church served by Pastor Ezra Stone, Icolyn had no difficulty in directing him to the Regal Community Centre in Ridgefield Road where he held his services. Pastor Stone returned the favour by visiting Icolyn and talked about the church and his ministry. He came to live in the area and had six children of his own, and it wasn't long before the two families became friends. Then quiet, 15-year old Blossom, who had been searching for a spiritual home, announced that she was joining his church – the Church of God of Prophecy. The 'stranger' was a pastor himself and his son, Grady Reid, was to follow Ezra Stone as pastor of the Church in Oxford, and to help Icolyn in setting up the Soup Kitchen.

The Church of God of Prophecy had its origins in rural North Carolina where it grew rapidly and, in 1903, established a more formal base in Cleveland, Tennessee. This has now become the international headquarters of a denomination with over 1.5 million members in 123 countries. As a Pentecostal church it is part of a renewal movement aspiring to reflect the spiritual power of the Apostolic Age of the early Christian Church, taking Acts 1: 15–26 as their essential text. It believes in the absolute authority of biblical teaching and baptism by the Holy Spirit, empowering believers with the use of spiritual gifts, such as divine healing and speaking in tongues.

The doctrines of the Church include repentance, leading to salvation and sanctification, and the restoration of wrongs. Belief in the Second Coming, eternal life for the righteous and eternal punishment for the wicked are fundamental to the faith. It requires its members to abstain from intoxicating and addictive drink and other substances, including the smoking of tobacco; it upholds traditional values in family life and forbids membership of organisations involved in secrecy and oath-taking. The Church is sustained through tithes and expects its members to be supportive of one another and to their community, and to become its disciples in encouraging others to join their congregation. A verbal covenant visibly and publicly joins believers to the Church of God of Prophecy.

After their rejection by the mainstream churches serving the communities where they lived, it had become common practice for immigrants from the Caribbean to meet together in their own homes for prayer and worship. In 1953 a mission from Cleveland introduced the Church of God of Prophecy to Bedford and, during the years that followed, it spread to many other cities in the UK. The Church inspired an evangelical commitment and many responded to the calling with missionary zeal and with total disregard for the worldly concerns of domestic harmony and security of employment. Thus it was that Evangelist White took the Church of God of Prophecy to Bristol and, having done so, then to introduce it to Oxford.

She was succeeded by Pastor Ezra Stone, who Icolyn remembers as being particularly inspiring in introducing God. His message was 'God is there for you. Life's problems are there too but God helps you through them.' It was the kind of reassuring message that Icolyn needed and she soon became a regular member of his Church; she was baptised by full immersion in Reading. It was a spiritual conversion which Blossom describes as being nearly as dramatic as that of Paul on the road to Damascus. Always feisty, Icolyn made a conscious effort to avoid conflict and strong language; she also stopped smoking. It is difficult, now, to picture an argumentative, swearing, smoking Icolyn but that is how her children can still remember her.

That was in 1972 and she has been a faithful member of the Church ever since, hardly ever missing a Sunday service. Eric followed her into the Church in the following year and was baptised in the John Bunyan Baptist Church which was hired for the occasion. In 1977 she joined a group on a 10-day visit to Cleveland for a conference at the Church's headquarters. This was just twelve years after Icolyn's arrival from Jamaica; at the same time she was bringing up a family of six children, including Hilroy, and her ability to find the necessary resources is a measure of her commitment. In 1988 she went on a pilgrimage to Israel where she visited Jerusalem, Nazareth and Bethlehem; she also saw the Dead Sea and the Pillar of Salt into which, according to the Old Testament, Lot transformed his wife.

In the 40 years of her membership, the Church of God of Prophecy has changed its Oxford location from the original hall in Ridgefield Road to the John Bunyan Baptist Church, where problems in scheduling services sometimes led to difficulties, resulting in another move; this time to East Oxford Community Centre. Next it was to St Luke's Church in Temple Road, followed by the Asian Community Centre which was to feature so strongly in Icolyn's life. At last, in 2003 it moved again, to the premises it still occupies, Littlemore Community Centre.

The Church in Oxford is part of a national network administered by a Bishop as national overseer and through regional overseers. Links with the Church's origins in Cleveland have evolved towards those of friendship rather than leadership although much of its educational material is shared. Its members seek to 'love God with our heart, soul and mind and to love our neighbour as ourselves.' Its vision includes making disciples of all peoples of the world but it declares a passion for Christian unity. The Church urges its followers to recognise their spiritual gifts which they are then encouraged to use to minister within their neighbourhood. Their natural abilities are all part of God's work, as Icolyn clearly demonstrates.

The current pastor in Littlemore is Jennifer Stone. Although still part of the Church of God of Prophecy, she and her ministry team now call their church GAPC: the God And People Centre. It has a vision of 'A people-loving God, transformed by the Holy Spirit, serving the community'; and a mission of 'Releasing people to reach out to others with care by nurturing and developing a lifestyle of worship that would lead others to God.' In practice this manifests itself in a number of community projects including prayer meetings in local schools and collective worship. In addition, the Church collaborates with the Anglican, Catholic and Baptist churches in Littlemore in contributing to the social and spiritual wellbeing of the neighbourhood's residents.

Up to 30 people come to the Sunday morning service in Littlemore; most of them are regulars and, as in Coolshade, there are more women than men. Together they have built a strongly motivated, caring community whose members not only support each other, but others too who are known to be in need of help. The services themselves are joyful, participatory gatherings accompanied by live and recorded music. They begin with a Call to Prayer led by a member of the congregation who has been preparing for the honour for some weeks. This is followed by Praise and Worship, consisting largely of inspirational music and singing. Next comes the main part of the service – The Word in which members of the ministry team offer teaching, perhaps on the theme of 'What does the Bible have to say about . . .?' Sometimes a member of the ministry team then leads the congregation in prayers for the Church, community and for those known to be in special need. After the service there are tea, coffee and refreshments, and sometimes a meal which turns the religious experience into a social event that can last long into the afternoon.

Over the years Blossom and Icolyn have been joined by other members of the family. Gary uses his radio experience in ensuring the musical element runs smoothly; his wife, Yvonne, used to run the successful gospel choir and their son, Darius, while barely a teenager, become a Young Ambassador and took a lead in some of the music. In 2000 Icolyn started running the Children's Ministry, usually attended by around ten children. After prayer and worship in the adult service, the young ones play games while the older children are taught how to pray and are given readings from the Bible. Icolyn then takes them outside if the weather is fine to show them 'what God has made.' She then invites volunteers to 'close us in prayer'. Instantly, many hands are raised and the chosen small person proudly but stutteringly delivers a little prayer, made up on the spot.

16

My Daughter, Companion and Best Friend

Icolyn says that her husband, Eric, was so delighted to have a daughter that when he first held this mite of a baby in his hands he called her his 'beautiful little blossom'. So Blossom it was from that moment on, even though she was subsequently christened Pamela.

A lifetime later and half a world away, Blossom lives in Greater Leys. There is serenity about her, a calm unassuming acceptance that much of what happens in life, or does not happen, is outside her control. Such serenity usually comes from feelings of security which, for Blossom, are rooted in her faith. She remembers an inner spirituality throughout her childhood and she read the Bible from an early age; she still does.

But security was not something Blossom had grown up with. The family was still in Kingston when she was born; both her parents had to work hard to make ends meet and life was a struggle. It was a struggle for everyone and, although she would not have been aware of it at the time, there were parts of Kingston that were dangerous too. When she was only seven, Eric decided that the prospects were better in England, and for the next five years, Icolyn was left to bring up her four young children on her own. When she left to join Eric, the children went to live with their grandparents in Coolshade before making the same journey themselves. They were on their own; everything was unfamiliar including the long, cramped flight across the Atlantic and their landing in this cold, grey country. It must have been a very anxious time for them all.

Blossom was a pretty teenager as the 1960s turned into the 1970s. This was a good time to be young; the British music scene had burst upon the world and, with it, bright new fashions and the beginnings of liberation from traditional attitudes. A new culture of youth was having an influence on almost every aspect of everyday living. But at the age of 15, when most of her schoolfriends were interested in music, clothes and boys, Blossom went to church.

Most Caribbean children were brought up on the discipline of Sunday School but Blossom felt the need to make a lifetime commitment to The Lord. On her own, she went to the Church of God of Prophecy which, at the time, was based in the Regal Community Centre in Ridgefield Road. There she found a real welcome by the pastor, Ezra Stone and by other members of the congregation, some of whom were even younger than herself. At home she had to endure the teasing of her brothers who believed she would quickly give up, but they were wrong. Later on, Icolyn was to follow her example, then Eric; Gary joined the Church at an early age and now his son, Darius, goes there too.

Like Icolyn, Blossom was never happier than when in the kitchen. She remembers cooking yams over an open fire in the yard outside the house in Kingston, a very hazardous activity for such a little girl. But when she settled in Oxford she took up baking, a skill that was to become very useful later in her life. After her education at East Oxford Secondary School and the College of Further Education, Blossom became an auxiliary nurse at the Radcliffe Infirmary, staying with her unit when it moved to the John Radcliffe Hospital. Later, she became a carer in the Social Services but was forced to retire following a back injury.

For their first few years the Randolph Street house was home to a family of eight, six of whom were passing through the excitement and anxiety of growth from childhood to adolescence, and then to adulthood. Gradually the number reduced: Dawn and Hilroy were the first to leave; then in 1976 Eric died and Norman and George got married. Suddenly, the house must have seemed very empty; there was just Icolyn, Blossom, now aged 22 and nine-year old Gary. The house was too big for them and the character of Cowley Road was changing as homes built for families were taken over by students;

Blossom

they moved to Kilburn Road in Littlemore. Eventually the time came for Gary to get married and for the next ten years, Icolyn and Blossom lived together in contented companionship. But about Blossom, it is impossible not to ask a very impertinent question: how was it that no man had managed to make such an attractive, homely person his wife? It was not a question that bothered Blossom much. As far as she was concerned the answer was simple: 'One day God will find a husband for me.' And in 2000 He did.

It seems to have been almost pre-ordained. She had turned down many opportunities for marriage in the past but, having reached the age of 46, she had become accustomed to the routine of living with her mother in happy independence. However Icolyn had never stopped praying for the right man to come along for Blossom but then she suddenly felt that a message was reaching her: there was no more need for that prayer because a husband was on his way. This turned out to be Andrew Reid. He was a member of the Church of

God of Prophecy in Birmingham and, during a short stay in Oxford, he visited the local church where he met Blossom. While he was there an inner voice told him 'that's your wife.' Back in Birmingham he prayed for guidance because an earlier, long-term relationship had failed; then a friend told him of a vision she had had in which he found a wife in Oxford. In the meantime Blossom had decided that he was the right man for her, and they married in the following year.

Over the years she and Icolyn had grown so close that the separation was difficult for them both. Blossom tells of the desolation they both felt after Eric's funeral and how they were both sitting together in silence. Eventually Icolyn said 'have you got anything to say?' and Blossom replied 'no.' There was, of course, so much to say but no need to say it. They knew each other so well that they almost shared the same thoughts. They shared the same sense of humour too and, later, could sit, talk and laugh together for hours. And as the years passed by and routines established themselves it seemed as if that would be the way life would continue.

Both had busy professional lives as carers in the Social Services, made busier when Icolyn opened the Soup Kitchen. In the evenings Blossom went to night school to improve her skills in sugar craft. Her efforts to teach Icolyn how to knit saw only modest improvements but, with greater success, she taught her mother to drive; Icolyn passed her driving test at the age of 59, but only after many hours with Blossom, practising how to reverse. Blossom took up gardening and bought a greenhouse; together they went on outings to the Chelsea Flower Show, to Brighton and elsewhere. Icolyn was forever trying out new diets but food interested her too much; she was, after all, an excellent cook, and it did not take long for the diets to be abandoned. Of course there were moments when they needed only their own company and it would be Blossom who retired to her room. As she remarks with a laugh 'you can't make my mother do something she doesn't want to do.'

Throughout this time, and beyond, the Church was a crucial part of their lives. Blossom's involvement took her to hear concerts of gospel singing around the country and to youth camps organised by the Church of God of Prophecy. When she was younger she had always enjoyed these week-long adventures under canvas in an attractive rural location, but later she became a helper in the junior camp. Part retreat and part holiday, youth camps became a bonding experience for their young participants and helped cement their faith.

After their marriage Blossom and Andrew lived with Icolyn until they found a home of their own. And when they did so, for the very first time in her life, Icolyn was living on her own. Alone but never lonely because Blossom and other members of the family called in every day and the telephone was ringing continuously. And she liked Andrew; he proved to be a good husband to Blossom, attentive to his mother-in-law, and very hard-working. The three of them go on holiday together and the relationship has grown so close than Icolyn feels she has gained another son.

Andrew is a baker and it is symptomatic of the family culture that when his business premises were devastated by floods, everyone rallied round to help him back on his feet. He and Blossom now run a new bakery in Berinsfield.

17

Norman, George, Dawn and Gary

Blossom's place in Icolyn's life is depicted in the previous chapter but the bonds which hold the family together give each member a special place of their own. Norman had always known that, one day, he would become head of the family and even when he was embarking on a new life as an independent married man, he never forgot that his first duty was to care for his mother. It was, in fact, a responsibility that his brothers and sisters shared instinctively and a measure of how close the family remains is that everyone, apart from Dawn who lives in London, has a key to the door of Kelburne Road, and sees Icolyn most weeks. However, there is always the understanding that Norman who, inheriting his father's placid character, is confidante for the family and Icolyn's first line of support.

His first experience of family responsibility came when he was just 14. As the oldest in the family it was to him that George, Blossom and Dawn looked up when they felt so alone on their journey to the UK. They were unprepared for the cultural shock they quickly found in Oxford. Norman, George and Blossom went to East Oxford Secondary School where they were seemed to be sidelined from the educational opportunities that the school provided. There was prejudice, even among the teachers, but each of the children found ways of dealing with it.

Norman had decided on a career as an electrician so, at the age of 16, he went to the College of Further Education to learn the trade. He was taken on as an apprentice by Ilco but the company failed to honour its obligation to provide day release so that he could continue with his studies, although this seemed to be available to his white colleagues. In effect, he was employed as a full-time worker at an apprentice's wage so, after three years, he found a better-paid position with Plessey, installing telephone exchanges for the GPO, which involved travel over a wide area.

However, at the age of 21, the lure of good money, regular hours and work on the doorstep drew him, like so many others, to the Cowley car factories, then under the management of British Leyland. It was monotonous work and stressful when he first joined, because this was the period of confrontation and strikes. But Norman had found a side-line. His good looks had attracted the attention of a London modelling agency which found him advertising work and, later, as an extra at Pinewood Studios. Look carefully at the James Bond film *Live and Let Die* and you will see him as a bouncer; and *At the Earth's Core* he appears as a tribal warrior.

On 27 March 1976 he married Lorna and thanks to the family savings scheme to which they all contributed, he could afford the deposit on a house in Turner Close. Lorna was a nurse, and still is; they have four children – Craig, Samantha and twins Matthew and Cory – and all of them have university degrees.

Norman in his modelling days

After 17 years he had had enough of the production line at Cowley. Lorna had embarked on a part-time degree course at Brookes' University and Norman decided to return to his earlier career in communications. At night he studied electronics at West Oxford College in Witney and, after a few temporary jobs, his new qualifications got him work with Ericsson. Experience with this respected international company opened the door for work on communications systems for the Joint European Torus facility at Culham, where Eric had worked soon after his arrival from Jamaica, some 40 years earlier. It was a sensitive job requiring him to be vetted for a security pass by the Ministry of Defence.

This was an exciting time to be in the new, burgeoning electronics industry and other opportunities soon presented themselves. In 1995 he joined Virgin Media, initially to install domestic telephone and television systems and, later, broadband; eventually he became a service engineer, responsible for sorting out local problems with the complicated new technology.

Norman had always kept himself fit; he was a keen runner and played squash frequently. But in 2011 he suddenly become unwell. Lorna recognised the symptoms and her suspicions proved correct: it was prostate cancer. For Norman, the shock of this diagnosis and debilitating treatments that followed were compounded by his inability to continue working. During this difficult time Lorna's professionalism, care and understanding were of critical support. Instead of having to attend his GP's surgery for his blood tests and injections, Lorna was able to do all that for him at home, and she went with him on every appointment at the Churchill Hospital. He was also fortunate in having a sympathetic employer in Virgin Media which continued to pay him for the next two years. The cancer was caught in time but, for an active man, the enforced idleness was frustrating. But no-one in Icolyn's family is idle for long; as soon as he became well enough, Norman was helping out at the Soup Kitchen.

Within three months of Norman's marriage, George put down a deposit on a house, coincidentally in the same road as Norman, and married June. She and George have known each other since they were teenagers. June has worked in the health and education services, becoming a specialist in dyslexia and she serves on the Oxford Learning Disability Partnership Board. They have two daughters: Alison, who has a Masters Degree in Business and Economics; she works in the international division of McDonalds, the hamburger chain, and Natalie, who is a teacher. Whereas there is much of his father in Norman's character, there is a good share of Icolyn's in George. He was a pugnacious little schoolboy, always ready to fight his corner – or someone else's if necessary. As soon as he joined East Oxford Secondary School he was picked on by the school bully; it needed a few fights to establish the pecking order and then they

George with Gordon Greenedge and Viv Richards

became friends. It was this self-confidence that made him the genial, articulate man he is now.

Cricket is George's passion and he played in school teams in both Kingston and Oxford. One of his proudest moments was when his father was watching a match between Wycombe West Indies and the Oxford Caribbean Cricket Club and saw him take a dramatic catch from a 'silly' position close to the wicket. Later he was to captain the Oxford Caribbean Cricket Club himself and to organise a benefit dinner for Joel Garner after the West Indies played Oxford University. At 6ft 8ins, Garner – or 'Big Bird' as he was known, was one of the tallest bowlers of his generation and the power of his delivery made him statistically one of the most effective in test cricket. This was the first of a number of benefits George organised for visiting star cricketers including Gordon Greenedge, Viv Richards, Courtney Walsh and Clive Lloyd.

George maintains that he has had only two jobs. The first was at the printer, E.W. Morris, where he did an apprenticeship as a compositor. Preparing text ready for printing was an intricate craft, now lost to computers that can accomplish a day's work in seconds. Each character, and the spacing between it and the next one, and between each line, was moulded in hot lead; pages made up in this way were then inked and the impression transferred to paper in noisy, heavy printing presses. Later, George went to work in the darkroom where illustrations were chemically etched into printing blocks for insertion into the text prior to printing. He stayed with the company for 22 years.

In the meantime he helped out in youth clubs in Cowley and Blackbird Leys and, through his increasing involvement, earned a position of trust in both the young people he worked with, and if they got into trouble, with the police. He contributed to advisory panels on community policing and was often called by the police as an intermediary after the arrest of wayward youths who preferred George's impartial council to the outrage of their parents.

Such work required discretion, judgement and responsibility. It became widely recognised that George had these qualities and in

1983, Evan Luard MP nominated him to become a magistrate. When he was first appointed he was the youngest in the country and continued to serve for the next 15 years.

After a period of training George served on the bench as one of three lay judges who, working as a team, had to decide on the cases brought before them. Often the decision was to refer the case to a higher court, but for cases meriting sentences of less than three years, they could reach judgements themselves. For George, the most difficult and distressing cases were those involving children because of the risk of splitting the family. Sometimes, however, there was a good outcome. Years later he was thanked by a former trouble-maker to whom George had given a nine-month sentence; he said it was the best thing that had happened to him and he had become a reformed character.

Enabling staff to take time off is a problem for any employer but George had an enlightened boss at E.W. Morris who offered encouragement, even though it meant that he was away from the factory on Fridays, alternate Wednesdays, and when the court was under pressure, on other days too. Eventually, however, E.W. Morris was sold and the new management demanded total commitment of its staff. The atmosphere became acrimonious and George was given notice to leave. However, with the backing of his union, George took his employer to court; the tribunal found in his favour and E.W. Morris had to pay him a substantial sum.

Luck was on his side because that payment was the opportunity he needed to realise an ambition he had to run a bar, modelled on the American TV series, *Cheers*. He decided that, with the opening of the M40 and the expansion in its housing and businesses, Bicester was the place to be. There were the added advantages of having the US Air Force base at Upper Helford not far away and, even closer, the Ministry of Defence storage and distribution facilities where hundreds of service personnel were employed. In 1989 he acquired the freehold of a wine bar in the town centre, secured a late-night license and renamed it G's. Upstairs there was a restaurant serving Caribbean food, often prepared by Icolyn or Gary.

Before it opened there was little late-night entertainment in Bicester, and G's was an immediate success. Over time George's original concept changed with changing tastes; and the customers changed with the closure of Upper Helford and the MOD bases. G's no longer has a restaurant and is now a nightclub, with DJs playing music into the early hours at weekends. George remains the 'meeter and greeter' for which his outgoing personality is ideally suited.

Back in Kingston of the 1960s, one of Dawn's earliest memories is of George, who was always 'such a naughty boy', when he cut Blossom's neck with a knife – fortunately, a blunt one. It was just a prank but could have been very dangerous. To teach him a lesson, Icolyn marched him down to the police station where she persuaded the sergeant in charge to lock him up for a few hours. He learned the lesson.

The family's ties with Jamaica are felt mostly strongly by Dawn who hopes, one day, to be able to live there permanently. She has returned many times, usually staying with her Auntie Enid, now living in Portmore, between Kingston and Spanish Town. It is a neighbourhood partly sustained by house-shops which bind the community together and it is Dawn's ambition to live in one. She has also travelled the island extensively, has been to Coolshade, and feels more at home in its warmth and easy-going lifestyle than in cold, competitive Britain.

At the age of three she went to Waterhouse Basic School in Kingston, not long before her father left for England in search of work. Dawn was six when he returned for a few week's holiday, and she remembers being impressed by a tape-recorder slung from his shoulder.

Within two years Dawn was to be in Oxford herself, along with her two brothers and Blossom. The flight over was cold, crowded and noisy. In one of the meals served by the cabin crew she encountered cornflakes for the first time – served with hot milk. It disgusted her so much that she has not touched either cornflakes or hot milk ever since. When they arrived at Heathrow it was even colder, and raining; the children had never known cold before, and by the time they reached Oxford in Eric's Hillman Minx, it was dark. That was a Friday and on the Monday, while her brothers and Blossom were old enough to go to secondary school, she alone went to East Oxford Primary School. There she discovered that hers was almost the only black face and that discrimination by her teachers as well as the other children, was unrestrained. She was just eight years old.

Although she hated school, family life was always fun, even when the 'family' was greatly extended by several temporary members to whom Icolyn had offered her home. Until Gary was born she was the youngest and enjoyed the attention that attracted but, as she grew older, it became apparent that she had inherited her mother's small stature and strong will. Tensions and clashes with her siblings became increasingly frequent and Dawn often felt unfairly judged. The heightened emotions of adolescence increased the friction and after one tumultuous family row, 16-year old Dawn left home.

Dawn as a teenager

She went to London. London is not a safe place for a 16-year old girl without friends or a home. Fortunately she found an Alone in London hostel near King's Cross. This organisation is a haven for young people drawn to the city's bright lights, often in circumstances similar to Dawn's. It helped her confront the realities of her situation and look to the future; but above all it established her independence.

Since then Dawn has been a Londoner. She may have been a rebel, but she was resourceful. She has never been without work; in the early days it was in factories and shops – anywhere that offered her a job, but more recently she has been a care assistant. During the first few years she lived and worked all over the city and got to know it well but, in 1982, she took a flat in Deptford which has been her home ever since. Her partner at the time was Michael, father of Abna, a biblical name from the Old Testament, meaning King of Old, and Olanikie which, in the language of the Yoruba tribe in Nigeria, means Crowning Glory. Icolyn has reason to be very proud of them as her grandchildren. Michael no longer lives with Dawn but their friendship is probably stronger than ever.

Dawn considers herself to be the black sheep of the family and in some senses she is. The rift with the other members of the family she left in Oxford deepened in 1996 when, on returning from a trip to Jamaica, customs officers found marihuana in her suitcase. She bought it to sell in London, to put something aside for her growing children. It was a stupid thing to do; she admits that, but her motives were unselfish. Her sentence was suspended for two years.

Like many in her family, Dawn felt a spiritual calling, but hers reflected her Jamaican roots. Dawn is a Rastafarian, which she describes as a way of life, but which conflicts with her mother's fundamental Christian beliefs. Time is healing the familial wounds but, in Dawn, one cannot fail to recognise the fighting determination of Icolyn.

By the time that Gary was born, Dawn was already ten years old and Norman and George had left school. As the new baby in the household, it was his turn to be spoiled. He had an easier time of it at school than his brothers and sisters because there was, by then, a significant immigrant population in Oxford, and children were no longer as aware of colour differences as adults. In any case, he grew rapidly into the tall, broad and muscular man he is today – the only member of the family to resemble his father, and he could certainly look after himself if necessary. As he was growing up Icolyn was worried about him playing with his mates in the park across the road from Randolph Street – the only open place in the neighbour-hood, but a haunt of drunks and junkies. As far as Gary was concerned though, they were no trouble.

One of Gary's most treasured memories is of the chopper bicycle that Norman gave him after his father's death. It was red, the real business and the envy of his friends at East Oxford Primary School. As soon as he was old enough to do so he took on a paper round and, later, did some after-school hours work at Tesco. He completed his education at Cowley St John and left at 16 to work in the Co-op which, at the time, was located in Cornmarket Street in central Oxford. However, he had set his mind on becoming a chef and he was lucky enough to get a three-year apprenticeship at St Anne's College.

Various catering jobs followed: he was at Oxford Moathouse Hotel for three years; he worked in the canteen of Oxford University Press, in the Carmelite Priory in Boars Hill and at the John Radcliffe Hospital; in between times he was a relief chef for a Swindon-based contract caterer, often requiring him to work in unfamiliar kitchens and at short notice. By then, though, he had married Yvonne and needed more regular working arrangements close to where they lived in Bicester. An opportunity arose in Bullingdon Prison. This was catering on a grand scale; gravy was made in 25-gallon vats, stirred with a paddle; rice was cooked in batches of 25 kilograms; chickens were roasted in six ovens, hundreds at a time. But in a prison food is regarded as fuel, not something to be enjoyed, and Gary's attempts to improve the menu were rebuffed. After four years and an accident involving some heavily-laden trolleys, he decided it was time for a change. Fortunately, however, his experience was not wasted. He was often able to help George in G's and, of course, he continues to use his skills in the Soup Kitchen.

Gary in his professional capacity as DJG

In the meantime he had been running his own mobile discotheque. As a committed Christian he was taken on by Premier Radio, a Christian radio station in London. There was a period when, after a 12-hour shift at Bullingdon Prison, he would drive down to London to record the next day's breakfast show. At BBC Radio Oxford he presented the Urban Gospel Experience on Sunday nights until it became a victim of budget cuts and, as DJG he has been booked at venues as far apart as Seattle, Dublin and Monaco. You need self-confidence to be a DJ, a quality that Gary recognised as lacking in many young people, and he has been passing on his skills at local colleges and at MacIntyre School near Aylesbury, which provides care and support for children with learning disabilities.

In 1989 Gary met Yvonne in a youth camp run by the Church of God of Prophecy in Southampton and, two years later, Yvonne's brother, Rejust Campbell married them in his first such service as a newly-qualified pastor in the Church. Their gifted son, Darius, was born in 1998. Yvonne teaches hair-dressing and deals with much of the administration behind the scenes of the Soup Kitchen. She is devoted to Icolyn and calls her 'Mum'; it is an honour, she says, to be her daughter-in-law

18

Caring and Sharing

To an outsider, and even to those on the inside, the regular appearance of a two-course lunch, with choices, every Wednesday, and a lighter meal on Saturdays, is a clear demonstration of an efficient, well-run organisation. However, it is an organisation in which no-one gets paid and it is entirely dependent of the goodwill of its helpers and supporters. From the beginning stood the faithful members of the Church of God of Prophecy who have willingly helped it out of occasional financial difficulties. Without their intervention there have been times when closure seemed inevitable but, somehow, that crisis has always been averted. Yvonne, Icolyn's daughter-in-law has the explanation: 'That's just God.'

Much of the burden for keeping the Soup Kitchen solvent during those periods of uncertainly fell on John Stone who, until Yvonne took over in 2012, had been its treasurer. Well-meaning people like Icolyn, who give freely of their time are not always the best at keeping receipts and other evidence of expenditure, presenting quite a challenge to someone who had been trained in the disciplines of the spread-sheet and profit-and-loss account. In the 1990s grants were readily available to organisations helping the disadvantaged but the economic downturn led to austerity and cuts in public spending, and the Soup Kitchen became increasingly dependent on private donations to keep going. In 2012 the City Council withdrew the financial support it had given for the previous 20 years, suggesting that organisations like it encouraged dependency, rather than self-reliance, among Oxford's homeless. However, that was also the year in which Icolyn's appearance on the *Secret Millionaire* gave rise to a substantial cash injection and it was this temporary relief which precipitated a feeling that the opportunity must be taken to safeguard the Soup Kitchen's future.

From the very beginning the Soup Kitchen had been using the same bank account as the Church of God of Prophecy and Icolyn had become increasingly uncomfortable about this connection and the liability it placed on the Church's members. The arrangement also meant that independent fund-raising was complicated by the need to pay the proceeds into the Church's bank account. It was time for the Soup Kitchen to stand on its own feet.

It was decided to manage the Soup Kitchen's affairs through a registered charity. As a charity it would demonstrate that it has proper management controls and make it eligible for funding through more formal routes. And so began the lengthy process of complying with the requirements of the Charity Commission and opening a new bank account. Yvonne became the main driver, aided by Yvette Hutchinson, who was affiliated with the Church of God of

Margaret Butcher serving at the Soup Kitchen.
Photograph: Harriet Browse

Prophecy, whose work with the British Council made her familiar with bureaucratic procedures and the kind of paperwork which many find so tiresome.

Further expertise and commitment was found among the kitchen helpers. Marlon Naidoo, a businessman from South Africa had lost everything when his transport company collapsed but while he was getting back on his feet he used his time productively in the Soup Kitchen. He was able to use his experience to suggest how it could be future-proofed against the kind of difficulties he had experienced. It was he who proposed that the charity should be called The Icolyn Smith Foundation in honour of the person who began it all. There was Margaret Butcher, who had met Icolyn while delivering the necessities of life to Oxford's homeless, part of a regular collection by members of her church, Trinity Church in Abingdon. Margaret was so inspired by the work of the Soup Kitchen that she became a loyal helper and a trustee of the Foundation. She was joined by Leif and Petronella Rasmussen, also from Trinity Church who, after hearing Icolyn speak at one of its morning services, also joined the team of helpers in the Soup Kitchen.

The congregation on that occasion was so moved by Icolyn's story of the plight of those that she and her helpers served that she was invited to address members of the Baptist Church in Abingdon as well, and it was there that Jenny Kain met her. Jenny has since become a regular helper. She and her husband took it upon themselves to use their pensions for buying cast-off clothes at jumble sales to give to those who come to the Soup Kitchen; dispensing them to those who need them most has become Jenny's special responsibility.

Another of the speakers at Trinity Church was Nancy Hunt, originally from Kenya. She came to talk about the Nasio Trust, a charity she runs with her husband and several others. The story began in 2000 when Nancy's mother heard a baby boy crying, and apparently abandoned, in a field of sugarcane. Unable to find who he belonged to, she took him in herself. He was soon joined by several more who were given an education, medical care and a daily

Icolyn with a photograph of Charles

meal in a roadside shack; all of them had been orphaned by HIV/ AIDS. Their number has now grown to over 300 in two day care centres. They are funded through sponsorship and other events organised by the Nasio Trust, which has its base in Abingdon. Locally, the Trust works with the police, army and schools in a programme called Exit 7, named after the seven types of antisocial behaviour which can result in an ASBO penalty for young people. They become involved in positive activities, career development and fund-raising, culminating in the opportunity to do voluntary work in Kenya; it has transformed the lives of many in the Abingdon area and turned them into useful members of society.

The Trust's many sponsors include Leif and Petronella, and Margaret, and they have all made the trip to Kenya in support of its work. Icolyn was so impressed by what the Trust achieves that, in 2013, she took the decision to become a sponsor as well. As a result she 'adopted' Charles, just ten years old at the time, both of whose parents had died of AIDS. She now gets an annual photograph of him and a school report; in return she sends him presents and pays £10 a month towards his upkeep and education.

About him Icolyn says 'I don't have much but at least I can share what I have.' It seems to sum up her life.